S0-FCZ-786

THE WORSHIP HANDBOOK

*A Practical Guide to
Reform and Renewal*

Thomas Anderson Langford, III

Musical Contributions by
Bonnie S. Jones

DISCIPLESHIP RESOURCES   NASHVILLE

ISBN 0-88177-011-6

Library of Congress Card Catalog Number: 84-70648

CONTENTS

I. REFORM AND RENEWAL
OF WORSHIP

Worship: Words, signs, and actions between the Word of God and human life in which people honor God and God makes people holy.

The single most important ministry of the church is worship. On Sunday mornings and other special days, more people, more expectantly, come to worship than to any other activity of the church. This handbook is intended to enable pastors and musicians, especially in The United Methodist Church, to minister more fully through worship.

Worship furnishes pastors and musicians their greatest opportunity for ministry. A good Sunday morning service, a reverent funeral, a celebrative wedding, or a joyous hymn festival can provide an occasion in which God and people become one. There is no greater joy than to lead and to participate in a good service of worship. This handbook describes ideas that will help make worship a vehicle of God's grace.

Yet worship is also a major task (and even, at times, a burden) for church leaders. At least once every week, and often more frequently, pastors and musicians must plan for worship. There are scripture lessons to choose, sermons and prayers to prepare, music to learn, hymns to pick, and new services to explore. Planning requires a large investment of time, energy, and creativity. This handbook will outline ideas that can help in all aspects of planning worship. Not all of these ideas can or should be used in any one church. But they have all been used in congregations and found practical.

Now is an auspicious time for leaders of worship to plan and work on worship. A religious revival is sweeping The United Methodist Church. New vigor inspires the denomination. The vigor of a United Methodist revival is most evident in United Methodist congregational worship.

During the first seven decades of the twentieth century, American Methodists worshiped in distinctive ways. The typical Sunday service of worship, with minor changes from time to time, consisted of prayers, collects, psalms, creeds, scripture readings, and hymns, followed by a hymn, sermon, hymn, and benediction. This Sunday service was an uneasy union of an Anglican "Morning Prayer" service, emphasizing prayer and meditation, and a Free Church revivalistic service, focusing on sermon and song. Methodists baptized and received the Lord's Supper using evangelically abridged services from the Church of England's

1

Book of Common Prayer. Distinctive Wesleyan services—Watchnights, Love Feasts, Covenant Services, and Song Services—also punctuated the worship life of each congregation. Despite conflicts between the styles of devotion evident in each service, and between different services, these patterns served well for many years. As a result, they dominated the 1965 *Book of Worship* (Nashville: Methodist Publishing House) and the 1966 *Book of Hymns* (*The Methodist Hymnal,* Nashville: Methodist Publishing House).

The way United Methodists worshiped, however, came under intense review. Beginning with the 1972 publication of *The Sacrament of the Lord's Supper, An Alternate Text* (Nashville: United Methodist Publishing House), and supported by the Section on Worship of the Board of Discipleship, United Methodists reevaluated their worship. They asked whether their patterns of worship were consistent with the best insights of the ecumenical church and of the United Methodist (or Wesleyan) tradition.

Many Christian communions had earlier altered their worship. Beginning with the Roman Catholics, and followed by the Lutherans, Anglicans, and other communions, many Christians worshiped in services adapted from the first three centuries of the church. The services for Sunday morning, the sacraments, and other occasions were focused on the Word of God and were simpler, with balanced form and freedom. The new services signaled new life in the ecumenical church.

United Methodists discovered that these ways of worship were consistent with the worship emphases of John Wesley in three respects: First, Wesley emphasized the Word of God. He always affirmed that scripture was the core of Methodist worship. Yet the traditional patterns of United Methodist worship had used only isolated bits of scripture, which were not at the heart of the services. Second, Wesley argued that worship should conform to the practices of the early church. Wesley sought a return to the simplicity of patristic worship. Yet the traditional United Methodist pattern was a complicated union of Anglican and Free Church practices. And third, Wesley advocated a balance between rigid orders of worship and liturgical freedom. The ideal style of worship combined spontaneous actions within an established structure. But most United Methodists worshiped exclusively with set patterns. These three principles—scripture, simplicity, and balance between form and freedom— called into question the older United Methodist patterns.

A Wesleyan revival in United Methodist worship then began. Through an appreciation of ecumenical liturgical advances and the rediscovery of Wesley's principles, United Methodists transformed their worship. The theology and practice of our worship have changed more in the last fifteen years than in the previous two hundred years. First, there has been a vigorous *reform* of the patterns and style of United Methodist worship. There are now alternative forms for United Methodist worship that emphasize the Word of God, a simpler pattern, and freedom within form. These alternative ideas are found in the fifteen volumes of the *Supplemental Worship Resources* series. They are:

The Sacrament of the Lord's Supper, An Alternate Text 1972 (Revised 1981) (SWR 1)
A Service of Baptism, Confirmation, and Renewal: An Alternate Text 1976 (SWR 2)
Word and Table: A Basic Pattern of Sunday Worship for United Methodists (Revised 1980) (SWR 3)
Ritual in a New Day: An Invitation (SWR 4)
A Service of Christian Marriage (SWR 5)
Seasons of the Gospel: Resources for the Christian Year (SWR 6)
A Service of Death and Resurrection (SWR 7)
From Ashes to Fire (SWR 8)
At the Lord's Table (SWR 9)
We Gather Together: Services for Public Worship (SWR 10)
Supplement to the Book of Hymns (SWR 11)
Songs of Zion (SWR 12)
Hymns from the Four Winds (SWR 13)
Blessings and Consecrations (SWR 14)
From Hope to Joy (SWR 15)

The patterns outlined in this series have not yet become the definitive forms of United Methodist worship, but they provide the foundation for the reform of United Methodist worship. Yet changes in United Methodist worship are not an end unto themselves.

The goal of the reform of United Methodist worship is worship *renewal*. Renewal takes place when worship becomes the center of the life of each Christian and each congregation. John Wesley always practiced his faith through worship. The Methodist revival prospered because of its rich worship. The same may also be true today. Worship may enable each Christian to express personal faith and experience the presence of God. And worship may also enable each Christian to grow in faith and grace in a community of faith. The goal of worship reform is to renew Christian life through worship.

The purpose of the handbook is to aid in the reform and renewal of worship in The United Methodist Church. It offers very practical suggestions to help leaders of worship plan services of worship. In addition, space has been left for the reader to add insights and ideas. The handbook's goal is to make worship the single most important ministry of the church.

The authors are indebted to many people for the ideas in the handbook. Dr. Don Saliers and Dr. Dennis Campbell encouraged its work and completion. Dr. Will Willimon, Dr. James White, Dr. Doug Adams, Dr. Hoyt Hickman, and the members of the Fellowship of United Methodists in Worship, Music, and the Other Arts provided many of the suggestions. Two books in particular undergird the theology expressed, though not stated, in the handbook: Dr. White's *An Introduction to Christian Worship* (Nashville: Abingdon, 1980) and Dr. Willimon's *Worship as Pastoral Care* (Nashville: Abingdon, 1979). We recommend these two books for leaders of worship who seek more insight into the reform and renewal of worship. And we especially thank all the Christians and congregations who have worked with us to explore and to write about worship.

Through the reasoned and pastoral use of this handbook, leaders of worship may help their congregations rediscover vital worship. And the faithful worship of God by each person and congregation may enable all Christians to express love of God and neighbor, and to be formed in faith and to grow in grace.

II. SUGGESTIONS FOR CONGREGATIONAL WORSHIP

As pastors and musicians plan for congregational worship, three basic ideas are critical: be biblical, be simple, and balance form and freedom. The Word of God gives the basic emphasis and flow to each service of worship. A simple service allows the Bible to speak to people and for people to respond to the Word unencumbered by peripheral words and actions. And the form of worship provides only a general shape to the service, allowing the Holy Spirit to infuse worship. These three elements are at the heart of the reform and renewal of United Methodist worship.

The following four principles will guide those who plan and lead worship in implementing the above suggestions:

1. Begin with the Bible. The Word of God establishes the core of the worship service. Ask, "What does the scripture say?"

2. Then identify the central realities of human life confronted by the scripture. Always ask, "What does this Word say to me and to my people?" "Where does the Word expose hurt?" "Where does the Word offer help?" The discovered realities of human life—joy, pain, life, death—then become the central thrust of the service.

3. And next, order the words, signs, and actions of worship around the scripture and human response, balancing form and freedom. Avoid being too thematic, rationalistic, pragmatic, complex, or bound to any one pattern of worship. But let every worship service be logical, clear, and progressive. Every service should have an easily discernible pattern, and the order must facilitate the dialogue between the living Word of God and the congregation's deepest needs.

4. Finally, having listened to the Word, having determined people's needs, and having chosen the appropriate pattern, let worship include all the people and all their senses. *Liturgy* is the Greek word for the "work of the people." Good worship, therefore, includes children, youth, and adults of all ages, races, sexes, and abilities. And good worship involves all our senses. Let the music, the movement, and the environment of worship amplify, expand, and enrich the dialogue between God's Word and human life.

```
        GOD'S  ◄─────────────►  HUMAN
        WORD        WORSHIP        LIFE
```

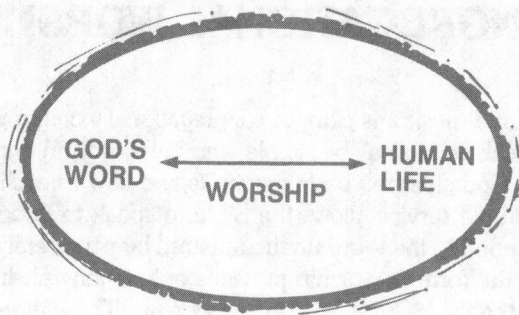

The remainder of this handbook elaborates upon the general suggestions made above by describing services of and suggestions for worship that are biblical, simple, and balanced. The following pattern outlines these services and suggestions.

1. The church year, grounded on the Word of God, provides the broadest structure for Christian worship. As the year develops, congregations hear from the written Word the whole gospel, from the anticipation and birth of the Messiah to the creation and ministry of the church. The lectionary, a series of three scripture readings for each Sunday and festival of the church year, is the best possible guide to the use of the Bible. But leaders of worship are not bound to the lectionary and may choose other scripture lessons that they believe are appropriate. Whether leaders use the lectionary or not, however, they should employ the Bible and let the services be shaped by the church year.

2. The basic pattern of each service of worship, found in *We Gather Together,* outlines the essential elements for each worship service: Entrance and Praise, Proclamation and Praise, Responses and Offerings, and Sending Forth. Other orders of worship may also be appropriate on any given day. But whatever pattern is used, the basic dynamic of worship in the life of each Christian and each congregation should be hearing and responding to the Word of God.

3. The sacraments of baptism and the Lord's Supper are central to the Christian life and are the highlights of corporate worship. Their use is fundamental to worship.

4. Numerous occasional services punctuate Christians' worship. Weddings, funerals, revivals and preaching missions, Wesleyan services, and other special services celebrate specific moments of Christian life.

5. Music in worship is among the richest of worship expressions. The appropriate use of hymns and anthems, the introduction of new music, and the creative use of music all enrich the spiritual life of the whole congregation.

6. Children in worship learn the good news of Jesus Christ and teach others the great tidings. They must be involved in every expression of worship.

7. Movement in worship enhances the dialogue between God and the people. Leaders and congregations at worship express their faith through their actions.

8. The environment of worship adds to the whole sensory experience of worship. The use of sights and smells sets the appropriate mood of worship.

Let us now examine and illustrate each of these eight aspects of worship.

III. THE CHURCH YEAR

Based on the Word of God read from the Gospels, Epistles, and Old Testament, the church year provides the large pattern for Christian worship. The year unfolds the full story of God's mighty acts with people and incorporates people into God's kingdom.

The year rests on two cycles baed on the Gospel readings. The first, yet lesser, cycle is Advent/Christmas/Epiphany. This cycle narrates the anticipation, birth, and manifestation of Jesus Christ. The most holy cycle is Lent/Easter/Pentecost. This cycle tells of the Lord's anticipated glory, the resurrection, and the creation of the church.

The Epistle lessons, read sequentially from the early church letters, remind the church of its early life and theology. These lessons may or may not be related to the Gospel lessons.

The lessons from the Old Testament in the present lectionary (found in *seasons of the Gospel*) are lessons that correspond to the Gospel lessons. In the Common Lectionary (chosen by the Consultation on Common Texts and to be introduced January 1, 1985) the lessons from Advent to Trinity Sunday remain the same. Then the lessons after Trinity Sunday, in subsequent years, tell the stories of the patriarchs and Moses (Year A), David (Year B), and Elijah, Elisha, and the minor prophets (Year C). The comments in this handbook reflect the new lectionary. See also *Introducing the New Common Lectionary* by Richard Eslinger (in the Worship Alive Series from Discipleship Resources).

Each of the lessons, having integrity of their own, must be studied separately and then brought together for the service of worship.

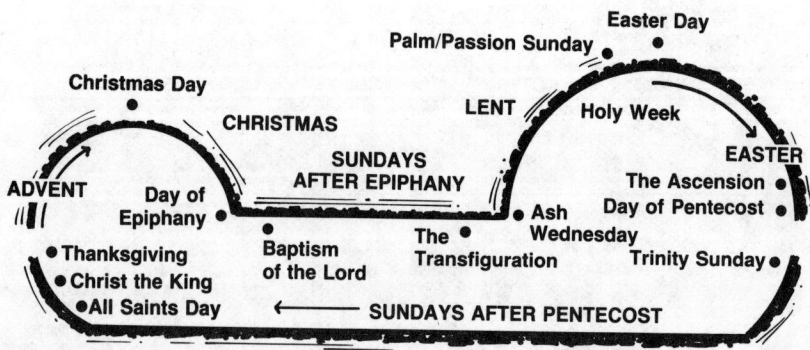

8

A. EACH YEAR

Leaders of worship—all ministers, musicians, choir directors, singers, ushers, readers, acolytes, altar guild members, worship committee members, and communion stewards—and the congregation review the liturgical highs and lows of the previous year. Fall is the ideal time for a review.

Leaders together then outline the broad goals for the upcoming year. See "Preparation for Change" (Chapter XI) for suggestions.

Worship leaders, especially ministers, note which books of the Bible are central each year and review those books.

- Year A (Advent 1986 to Season after Pentecost 1987)—Matthew, Romans, 1 Thessalonians, 1 Peter, and Old Testament lessons about the patriarchs and Moses.

- Year B (Advent 1984 to Season after Pentecost 1985)—Mark, 2 Corinthians, 1 John, Hebrews, James, and Old Testament lessons about David.

- Year C (Advent 1985 to Season after Pentecost 1986)—Luke, 2 Thessalonians, 1 and 2 Timothy, Philemon, Galatians, Philippians, Colossians, and Old Testament lessons about Elijah, Elisha, and the minor prophets.

Valuable homiletical studies for the church year include the 9-volume series *Preaching the New Common Lectionary* (Nashville: Abingdon), the *Knox Preaching Guides* (not yet completed; Atlanta: John Knox Press), *Proclamation Commentaries* (54 volumes in paperback; Philadelphia: Fortress Press), *Interpretation Series* (not yet completed; Atlanta: John Knox Press), Reginald Fuller's *Preaching the Liturgical Year* (Minnesota: Liturgical Press, 1974), and D. T. Hessel, *Social Themes of the Christian Year* (Philadelphia: Geneva Press, 1983).

B. EACH SEASON

Good leaders of worship plan well in advance of each church season, at least two or three months prior to use. They know their goals and aims for the upcoming season. This planning involves all worship leaders—ministers, musicians, choir directors, singers, ushers, readers, acolytes, altar guild members, worship committee members, and communion stewards. Together they will:

1. Review all the lectionary readings or other scripture readings for the whole season. Study *Preaching the New Common Lectionary, the Knox Preaching Guides, Proclamation Commentaries, Interpretation Series,* or *Preaching the Liturgical Year* to help develop larger themes. Then outline the general themes of the scripture.

2. Outline the general human realities spoken to by the Word.

3. Make initial preparations for special services, sermons, new hymns and music, special movements, and environmental changes. Be sure to coordinate all church activities—newsletters, bulletins, study groups, and special emphases—with the church year, not the calendar year. For example, send out a newsletter for Advent/Christmas/Epiphany rather than for November, December, and January. Let the confirmation classes follow and work through the church year from Advent to Pentecost.

Note well: In each season, the Word of God, whether taken from the lectionary or not, takes priority. Then the leaders of worship determine how to lead human responses to the Word. Prayer and song are the primary actions of the people. Then leaders choose special services, actions, and settings. Always focus first on the Word, then response, and then let the other elements of worship enhance the dialogue between the Word and human life.

Based on this premise, the following suggestions for each season are presented, using this outline:

- Word of God
- Prayer
- Hymns, anthems, and special music. See chapter VII for specific suggestions on how to introduce new music to a congregation, how to use music creatively, and for ideas for anthems and other special music. Throughout the handbook the following abbreviations will signify United Methodist hymnbooks:
  BOH   *Book of Hymns*
  SBOH   *Supplement to the Book of Hymns*
  SOZ   *Songs of Zion*
  CEL II *Celebremos II*
  HFFW   *Hymns from the Four Winds*
- Special Services
- Signs

- Colors. See chapter X for specific suggestions on how to arrange the environmental signs and colors of worship.

C. ADVENT: "CHRIST IS COMING"

Advent is a season of four Sundays and four weeks. *Advent* from the Latin *Adventus* means "coming." Begin the season with an Advent Festival or Fair to help a church and families prepare the church and homes for the season.

See *From Hope to Joy* (Nashville: Abingdon, 1984). This new resource outlines suggestions for the Sundays preceding Advent, the services of Advent, Christmas, and Epiphany, and for the Sundays after Epiphany.

Also see Vincie Allessi's *Programs for Advent and Christmas* (Valley

Forge, PA: Judson, 1978) and Donald and Patricia Griggs' *Teaching and Celebrating Advent* (Nashville: Abingdon, 1981).

Word of God

The Sundays of Advent emphasize the following themes in the same order each year: consummation of the coming of the King, John the Baptist, John the Baptist and Jesus Christ, and preparation for the birth of Christ. These readings focus on the anticipation of and preparation for Christ from the synoptic Gospels (Matthew, Mark, and Luke), John, Isaiah, and Revelation.

They do not focus on the Christmas story itself. Wait until Christmas to tell of Christ's birth.

Note the tension between the birth and the return of Christ. This is a good time to proclaim the return of the Lord and the expectation of a new King.

Prayer

Emphasize prayers of confession. See the Advent prayers in *The Book of Hymns*, 676ff. See the prayers in *The Book of Worship*, pp. 66ff.

Hymns

Music in Advent is difficult to choose. Most congregations want to begin singing Christmas carols as soon as they are heard in the department stores and when Christmas decorations begin to appear.

More appropriately, however, Advent worship should emphasize the singing of Advent hymns. These hymns do not celebrate the birth of Christ as do the Christmas carols and hymns. Rather, they tell of the coming of and the preparation for the Messiah.

Most congregations do not know many Advent hymns. Therefore, it will be a process of education and understanding. But by learning well at least one new Advent hymn each year, a congregation will soon know and love these hymns.

Explain to the congregation why you are not singing Christmas carols through Advent. There will probably be resistance to this change. You can sing some carols closer to Christmas.

Use one Advent hymn as the "Hymn of the Month" to be sung each Sunday through Advent so that the congregation becomes familiar with this hymn. (See Introducing New Hymns, after "New Hymns" in chapter VII.)

Interpret an Advent hymn by a banner and use the hymn theme or focus throughout Advent. For example, choose "Come Thou Long Expected Jesus" #360 BOH; use the word *Come* on the banner, and each week add something new from the hymn: hope, joy, release, deliverance.

Have the congregation sing just a portion of an Advent hymn for the introit:

BOH #354	"O Come, O Come Emmanuel," Latin, 12th century
BOH #359	"Hail to the Lord's Anointed," Montgomery
BOH #356	"Break Forth, O Living Light of God," Christierson
SBOH #963	"The King of Glory Comes," Jabusch, folk tune, hand clapping

Use "Watchman, Tell Us of the Night," #358 BOH. Sing antiphonally in the question-answer form: choir sing the first line, the congregation respond with the second line, third is choir, fourth is congregation.

Use hymns with a sense of expectation of hope that fits with the Word as preached that day. Some suggestions:

BOH #362	"There's a Voice in the Wilderness Crying," Milligan. Use when emphasizing the role of John the Baptist.
BOH #354	"O Come, O Come, Emmanuel," Latin. Ancient plainsong melody. Give background of this kind of music, which was used by the Christian church for 1500 years.
BOH #357	"Of the Father's Love Begotten," Prudentius. Ancient plainsong. Give background of plainsong as above.
SBOH #941	"On Jordan's Banks the Baptist's Cry," Coffin. Use when emphasizing the role of John the Baptist.

Special Services

See *From Hope to Joy* for a series of special services.

Celebrate Communion on the First Sunday of Advent. Use the full service, *Holy Communion*, found in BOH #830. This ritual's penitential quality helps set a good tone for Advent.

Confirmation

Advent is an excellent time to begin a confirmation class. This time of preparation trains youth and adults to assume the full responsibility of Christian discipleship.

See "Baptism" (Chapter V) for a full discussion of this new pattern of confirmation training.

Confirmation During Advent:

Begin the confirmation training with a service of dedication of the candidates on the First Sunday of Advent. Use Wesley's "Covenant Renewal Service" (Chapter VI).

Ask the confirmands to read weekly the lectionary readings for Advent.

Ask the candidates to pray daily for one-half hour.

Pray for the catechumenates by name during each worship service.

Encourage the candidates to read the lessons during worship each week, and to lead in prayer. Use them especially during the special services of Christmas.

Signs

Ministers and choirs wear black robes.

Use ausfere and simple settings.

Light an Advent wreath. The wreath is a circle of four candles (red, or purple, or three purple and one pink candle) with a center white candle. The wreath may be placed on the table or hung from the ceiling. Each week in Advent, one additional candle is lit, until Christmas Eve, when the center candle is also lit.

Set up a chrismon tree. This is an evergreen tree covered with white monograms of Christ, such as a star. Let the whole congregation decorate the tree. Save the chrismon trunk to make a cross for Lent.

Special signs that may be appropriate for the communion table: root of Jesse, plumb line of Amos, trumpets of Isaiah, star of David, messianic rose, blooming desert, desert scene, tree of Jesse, star of Jacob, fleur-de-lis.

For several booklets about chrismons and how to make them, write the Lutheran Church of the Ascension, 314 West Main Street, Danville, Virginia 29541 (also available from Cokesbury). See also *Symbols of His Coming: Four Chrismon Programs,* by Marian Gannaway, in the Worship Alive series, Discipleship Resources.

Colors

Use the more somber colors of purple, blue, or gray. Emphasize cloth with a rough texture. These somber rough colors are used for paraments (cloth decorating the church), stoles (cloth worn over the shoulders of worship leaders), and banners (cloth hangings).

D. CHRISTMAS: "JESUS CHRIST IS BORN"

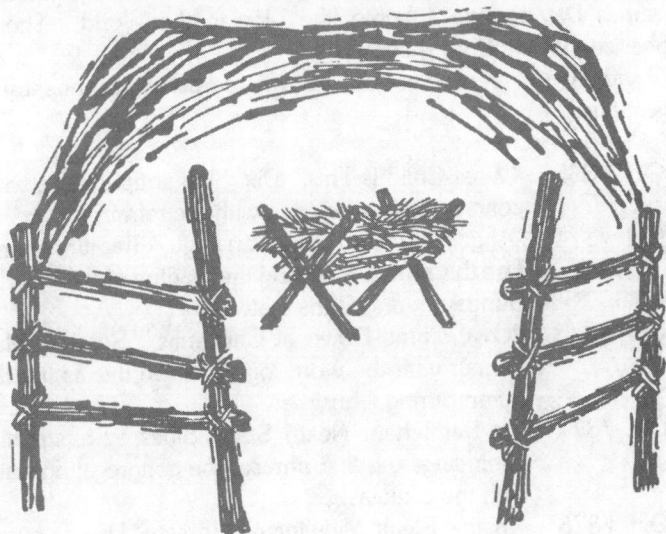

Christmas is a season that begins with Christmas Day and continues through the Day of Epiphany. The name *Christmas* comes from the season's first service, the Christ Mass. *Epiphany* comes from the Greek *epiphaneia* which means "manifestation."

Do not begin the season too early or end it too quickly.

See *From Hope to Joy.*

Word of God

Concentrate on the birth narratives emphasizing the incarnation.

Tell the Christmas story.

Sing the hymn setting of Zechariah's Benedictus, found in the *Book of Hymns*, #666.

Emphasize the magi (wise men) on the Day of Epiphany.

Prayer

Emphasize prayers of celebration, not confession.

See the *Book of Hymns*, #682ff, for Christmas prayers.

See the prayers in the *Book of Worship*, pp. 71ff.

15

Hymns

All congregations enjoy singing Christmas carols. After singing Advent hymns through Advent it is thrilling to *wait* until Christmas Eve or Christmas Day to sing a hymn like "Joy to the World." Then you emphasize that the *Lord is come!*

For variety and creative use of Christmas carols and hymns, try these suggestions:

BOH #385   "What Child Is This," Dix. Sing antiphonally, with the congregation answering with the refrain.

BOH #374   "Angels We Have Heard on High," Traditional French. Use this refrain following the reading of the Word each Sunday during Christmas.

BOH #375   "Love Came Down at Christmas," Rossetti. Make a banner with the word *love* and use this as the theme hymn during Christmas.

BOH #377   "In Bethlehem Neath Starlit Skies," Stutsman. The choir sings the first phrase, the congregation answers with the alleluias.

BOH #376   "In the Bleak Midwinter," Rossetti. Use as a prayer response.

BOH #386   "O Come, All Ye Faithful," Latin hymn. Use as hymn of gathering each Sunday of Christmas season. Use different stanzas each Sunday.

BOH #394   "While Shepherds Watched Their Flocks," Tate. Sing all stanzas to tell the full story.

SBOH #978   "Who Is He in Yonder Stall," Hanby. Sing question and answer antiphonally.

SOZ #2   "Glory Be to Our God on High," James. Use through Christmas season as hymn of praise or petition.

SOZ #75   "Go, Tell It on the Mountain," Traditional.

See the excellent indexes in HFFW and SBOH for Christmas hymns and carols.

Special Services

See *From Hope to Joy* for some beautiful special services.

Celebrate Christmas Eve with a service of candles and carols. Let the confirmation candidates read the lessons. One possible service that follows this pattern is:

A Service of Lessons and Carols

Call to Worship
Lesson: Genesis 3:8-19
Carol: "O Come, O Come Emmanuel" BOH #354
Lesson: Isaiah 9:2-7
Carol: "The People That in Darkness Sat" BOH #361
Lesson: Micah 5:2-4
Carol: "O Little Town of Bethlehem" BOH #381
Prayers of Concern and Celebration
Offering
Doxology
Lessons: Luke 1:26-38
              Luke 2:1-14
Carols: "The First Noel" BOH #383
              "Hark, the Herald Angels Sing" BOH #388
Lesson: Matthew 2:1-11
Carol: "We Three Kings" BOH #402
Lesson: John 1:1-14
Carol: "Joy to the World" BOH #392
Benediction

Observe a Watch Night Service on Christmas Eve or at the end of the year. See the Wesleyan Services (Chapter VI) for suggestions. See the *Book of Worship*, pp. 77-81, for an appropriate service.

Celebrate Communion on Christmas Day. Use the Christmas Prayer of Great Thanksgiving found in *At the Lord's Table*.

Present a nativity drama.

Observe a Covenant Renewal Service on New Year's Day or on the Day of Epiphany. See the Wesleyan Services for suggestions. See *We Gather Together* for *A Service of Baptism, Confirmation, and Renewal* (Chapter V). These are excellent services to give strength to candidates for confirmation.

The Day of Epiphany is an excellent day for baptisms.

Celebrate Communion on the Day of Epiphany. Use the Prayer of Thanksgiving found in *At the Lord's Table*.

Signs

Ministers and worship leaders wear albs or white robes.

17

Keep the Christmas symbols up through the Day of Epiphany, especially the chrismon tree. A great festive occasion may be a community burning of Christmas trees on the Day of Epiphany.

Hang a Christmas star.

Place evergreen wreaths on church doors.

Use poinsettias and roses.

Set up a crèche (nativity scene). But do not include the magi until the Day of Epiphany.

Colors

Use white and gold.

The cloth for paraments, stoles, and banners should be of finest texture.

E. SUNDAYS AFTER EPIPHANY: "CHRIST IS THE LIGHT OF THE WORLD"

A season of ordinary Sundays, beginning with the baptism of Jesus and ending with the transfiguration of the Lord. A season in which to slow down until Lent.

See *From Hope to Joy* for suggestions.

Word of God

The season is full of little epiphanies (manifestations), such as Christ's baptism, the miracle at Cana, and the transfiguration.

Prayer

Prayers of praise and confession may be appropriate, depending on the human response to the Word for the day.

See the *Book of Hymns*, #686ff, for Epiphany prayers.

See the *Book of Worship*, pp. 82ff, for prayers.

Hymns

During the Sundays after Epiphany sing hymns about light, witness, and proclamation. This season of ordinary Sundays is a good time to teach new hymns. Some suggestions:

BOH #403　"Walk in the Light," Barton. Have the congregation sing a different stanza each Sunday as the introit or a response to prayer.

BOH #401　"Christ Whose Glory Fills the Skies," Wesley. One of Charles Wesley's greatest hymns. It is biographical of his own experience—darkness and joylessness until his conversion.

BOH #410　"We've a Story to Tell to the Nations," Nichol. Use as a hymn response to the Word either read or preached, using different stanzas.

SBOH #904　"I Come with Joy," Wren. A joyful folk tune that focuses on communion, presence, witness.

SBOH #948　"Peace I Leave You," Traditional. Sing this round as a benediction for witness.

SBOH #951　"Rise, Shine, You People." Klung. Use as a good anthem. Use banners, as it mentions "banners high unfurling."

SOZ #75 and	
BOH #404	"Go Tell It on the Mountain," Traditional. Use as a closing hymn of witness and sending forth.
CEL II #13	"The Lord Is My Light," Psalm 27:1, 14. Has a simple rhythm.
CEL II #25	"Give Us Your Light," Lockwood. Use as a solo or anthem.
CEL II #38	"I Am the Light of the World," John 8:12. May be combined in various ways, with calypso rhythm optional.
HFFW #52	"The Sun Is Rising O'er the World," Sambika. This is a wonderful text on Jesus as the Light of the world.

Special Services

Begin the season with a festive service of Christ's baptism. Celebrate Communion using the Prayer of Thanksgiving for the day from *At the Lord's Table.* An excellent day for baptisms.

End the season with a service celebrating the transfiguration. Celebrate Communion.

On the last day before Lent, hold a Shrove Tuesday Service. Serve a pancake dinner to use up butter and fats. (Also called *Mardi Gras,* or Fat Tuesday.)

Signs

Ministers and leaders of worship wear robes appropriate to the Word for each day of the season.

Place on the Communion table water jars for the miracle at Cana, or bright candles for the transfiguration.

Colors

White the first and last Sundays after Epiphany, green on the Sundays in between. With green and white, use contrasting colors on paraments, stoles, and banners to accentuate these more neutral colors.

F. LENT
"JESUS CHRIST SUFFERS AND DIES"

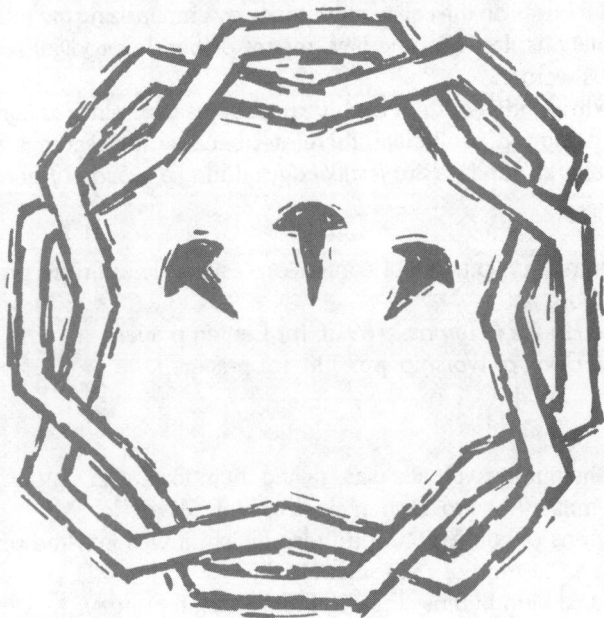

Lent is a season of forty days, not counting Sundays, that begins on Ash Wednesday and ends on Holy Saturday. *Lent* comes from the Anglo-Saxon word *leneten,* which means "spring."

From Ashes to Fire is the best available resource for worship during the great cycle of Lent/Easter/Pentecost.

See also Donald and Patricia Griggs' *Teaching and Celebrating Lent-Easter* (Nashville: Abingdon, 1982).

Word of God

Follow the lectionary. The readings concentrate not on mourning but on the anticipated glory of Jesus Christ that comes through suffering. Note well the use of the signs from the Gospel of John and the temptation of Jesus.

Year A focuses on divine encounters by emphasizing the following: the temptations, Nicodemus, woman at the well, man born blind, and Lazarus raised.

Year B focuses on the judgments of Jesus Christ by emphasizing the following: the temptations, rebuke of Peter, temple cleansing, judgment, and present judgment.

Year C focuses on the call to repentance by emphasizing the following: the temptations, last become first, repent or perish, prodigal son, and adulterous woman.

The sixth Sunday of Lent each year narrates the Palm/Passion story.

Avoid being too penitential, therefore, because the readings are not penitential and Sundays are *festival days* during a *season of penitence*.

Prayer

Concentrate on prayers of confession, especially after the preached Word of God.

See the *Book of Hymns*, #691ff, for Lenten prayers.

See the *Book of Worship*, pp. 90ff, for prayers.

Hymns

Avoid the hymns with alleluias, saving them for Easter.

Use hymns of the cross when close to Holy Week.

Use hymns of confession and those which fit well into the scripture readings and sermon of each separate day.

Use the passion hymns closer to Palm/Passion Sunday.

Consider Lent as a time of service to others, and use some of the mission hymns or hymns of service.

See the index of each worship supplement for the special emphasis you would like to make during the Lenten season.

Use hymns on prayer, for this is a season of prayer.

Spirituals focus on depth of spiritual life and hard trials. This is a good season to sing some of these suggestions:

SOZ #171	"Nobody Knows the Trouble I've Seen," Traditional.
SOZ #95	"I Want Jesus to Walk with Me," Traditional. Use as a solo on middle stanza and have the choir hum.
SOZ #133	"The Time for Praying," Traditional. Use as an anthem or solo.
BOH #124	"Ask Ye What Great Thing I Know," Schwedler. Use question and answer sung antiphonally.
BOH #183	"Must Jesus Bear the Cross Alone?" Shepherd. Use question and answer form. Sometimes have the question sung from the balcony or other parts of the church.

BOH #432   "What Wondrous Love Is This," American folk hymn.
Use with congregation, as an anthem, or with a solo
voice.

Special Services

Ash Wednesday

This service leads Christians to face their own sinfulness and mortality
in preparation for the mystery of redemption. The goal of the service is
not to be overly penitential, but to set the stage for spiritual growth by
recognizing our own need for salvation. This service sets the mood for
Lent.
See *From Ashes to Fire* for a full copy of the service.

A. *Entrance and Praise*

Silent meditation and prayer begin the service.
Set the sanctuary with no flowers, and focus on a large cross, crown of
thorns, or other Lenten symbol.
Ministers and worship leaders wear black robes.
Offer prayers of confession using sentence prayers, prayer requests, or
silent prayers.
Sing: BOH #432 "What Wondrous Love Is This," American folk
hymn.

B. *Proclamation and Praise*

Encourage the laity to read the lessons.
Follow lessons with time of silent meditation.
Use liturgical dance to illustrate the lessons.

C. *Responses and Offerings*

Minister calls the people to a Lenten discipline of examining self,
penitence, praying, fasting, giving, and reading scripture.
Imposition of the Ashes follows. Make ashes from burned palm
branches (from last year's Palm/Passion Sunday), chrismon tree or Advent wreath branches, or slips of paper bearing the confessions of the
people, and mix with oil. Make a sign of the cross with the ashes on the

23

forehead of each person who comes and kneels, saying: "Remember that you are dust, and to dust you shall return."

When all the people have received the sign of the cross, people respond with Psalm 51:1-17 (BOH #571).

The minister offers a prayer of pardon, reconciliation, or commendation.

D. Sending Forth

People leave in silence.

Also see the *Book of Worship,* pp. 90ff., for another Ash Wednesday Service.

After Ash Wednesday

On the first Sunday of Lent, use the full Communion order in the *Book of Hymns,* #830. This emphasizes the penitential quality of the season. Use the full musical setting for the Lord's Supper.

Or celebrate Communion using the Prayer of Great Thanksgiving for Lent in *At the Lord's Table.*

Encourage Lenten practices: fasts, prayer, intense devotion, and prayer.

Especially encourage the Lenten practices with the candidates for confirmation.

Encourage study groups during Lent. Study together the lessons for each week.

Lent, especially Holy Week, is the ideal time for a revival. See Revivals and Preaching Missions in Chapter VI.

Begin Lent with the excellent hymn, SBOH #937, "O Love, How Deep" (Latin) with the familiar tunes of BOH #21 or BOH #431.

Signs

Ministers and worship leaders may choose to wear black robes to emphasize the penitential nature of this season.

Create austere settings: costly perfume, coins, whip, crown of thorns, torn garment, nails, spear, sponge, broken reeds.

Avoid the use of fresh flowers.

Erect a large rough wooden cross (4' x 6') made from the chrismon tree.

Hang a gray or purple Lenten veil over the sanctuary cross.

Hang banners showing the stages of Christ's passion.

G. HOLY WEEK

While Holy Week is not a season (it contains services from both Lent and Easter), nevertheless Holy Week stands at the center of the church year. This week's services demand the greatest attention and work.

Especially read again *From Ashes to Fire*.

PALM/PASSION SUNDAY

The most dramatic of all the new orders of worship. Palm/Passion Sunday, formerly "Palm Sunday," is not the proper day either to baptize or to receive new church members. Nor is it the time for Easter cantatas or song festivals. Rather, this is the time to reenact in chronological order the story of Christ's final days.

See the service in *From Ashes to Fire*.

1. *Entrance and Praise*

Ministers and leaders wear black robes with stoles of Hosanna.

The sanctuary is set with palm leaves and a large rough cross. Emerald leaves may be substituted for palm leaves. Save the leaves for next year's Ash Wednesday service.

Set the table with bread and wine, coins, nails, spear, and water.

The congregation gathers outside or in a fellowship hall. From there the people hear the readings of Jesus' triumphal entry into Jerusalem. The congregation joins in a procession of palms.

2. *Proclamation and Praise*

Ministers and leaders change stoles to a more solemn color. Change the paraments and banners to bleaker colors of black or purple, made with cloth of rough texture.

Read the extended lectionary readings. Let readers from the choir or congregation read the whole passion narrative. Readers may dress in appropriate clothing. Scripts of the passion readings are found in *From Ashes to Fire. From Ashes to Fire* also describes other ways to read the passion story or to alternate readings with hymns. Ask candidates for confirmation to read the passion narrative.

3. *Responses and Offerings*

Responses to the Word may include the Lord's Supper (see the Palm/Passion Prayer of Great Thanksgiving in *At the Lord's Table*), an altar call, or a call to time of prayer.

4. *Sending Forth*

Leave in silence.

Hymns

Sing a triumphal song during the procession of palms. Suggestions:

BOH #424 "All Glory, Laud, and Honor," Theodulph of Orleans.
BOH #422 "So Lowly Doth the Savior Ride," Pennewell.
BOH #423 "Hosanna, Loud Hosanna," Threlfall.
BOH #425 "Ride On, Ride On in Majesty," Milman.
SBOH #900 and CEL II #37 "Hosana" (Mantles and Branches),
              Ruiz.

Consider having people in the corners of the sanctuary singing the part of the chorus "From every corner a thousand voices sing. . . ."

Sing a passion hymn following the scripture readings of passion.

Suggestion:

BOH #76 "At the Name of Jesus," Noel.

See indexes from BOH, HFFW, and the SBOH for hymns that fit appropriately with the scripture texts and sermon.

Do not return to a triumphal hymn at the close of the service. Stay with the theme of suffering death.

HOLY MONDAY, TUESDAY, AND WEDNESDAY

This is an excellent time for noontime services. See *From Ashes to Fire.*

Word of God

Follow the lectionary, recognizing that the way of the cross is the path to glory.

Use lay readers.

Prayer

Prayers should correspond to the scripture readings. Free prayer by the people is most appropriate.

Use directed or bidding prayers (prayers that ask people to call out silently or publicly personal concerns).

Hymns

Use the *Book of Hymns,* index #847, and the other indexes of the other hymn books to select hymns. Use hymns of the cross and of the passion. Consider using spirituals from *Songs of Zion,* which often describe suffering and pain.

Signs

Ministers and leaders wear black robes.

Continue to use the Lenten symbols: cross, costly perfume, coins, whip, crown of thorns, torn garments, nails, spear, sponge, and broken reed.

Avoid the use of flowers.

Emphasize fasts and almsgiving.
Employ liturgical dance.

Colors

Dark and solemn colors—red, blue, purple—are appropriate. Each day the colors should be more somber, using cloth overlays.

SEDER

The Seder, a Jewish family meal to remember the Egyptian captivity and the Exodus, may be celebrated in the church during Lent or Holy Week. One most appropriate time would be a church supper immediately preceding the Maundy Thursday service.

See *From Ashes to Fire* for one possible service that may be adapted for congregational use.

But be cautious that the celebration does not insult the integrity of Judaism. Rather, invite a Jewish family to come lead the congregation in the meal.

MAUNDY THURSDAY

A most holy service. The basic service includes six elements, which may take one and a half to two hours to observe fully.

Be clear that this service does not act out or repeat the Last Supper, but instead is a new service of Communion that is based on the Last Supper *and* the meals shared by the disciples and resurrected Lord.

Also avoid the dangerous custom of "drop in" Communion that denies the reality that the Holy Meal is a community act which unites God with people.

See *From Ashes to Fire* for a superior service.

See also the new rite for Maundy Thursday in *The Book of Common Prayer* (Seabury, 1979).

1. Introductory Rites

Emphasize repentance through silent prayer and corporate confessions.

2. Word of God

Follow the lectionary readings.
Use psalms sung as responses to the Word.
Hymn suggestions:

BOH #431 " 'Tis Midnight, and on Olive's Brow," Tappan.
BOH #436 and SOZ #126 "Were You There?" Traditional.
SBOH #914 "Jesu, Jesu," Colvin.
SBOH #976 "Where True Love and Charity," Proulx.
SBOH #978 "Who Is He in Yonder Stall," Hanby.

3. Footwashing

Make sound preparations by informing the people beforehand and providing adequate basins of water and towels.

Small churches may have each person participate. Large churches may let the pastor wash the feet of twelve selected people.

4. Holy Communion

See the Prayer of Great Thanksgiving for Maundy Thursday in *At the Lord's Table*.

5. Stripping of the Church

Remove all religious objects from the sanctuary.

6. Tenebrae

Extinguish thirteen large lighted candles as the passion narrative is read. *From Ashes to Fire* gives several ways to read the story.

There are musical settings for the Tenebrae service for choir. Example: *Service of Darkness* by Dale Wood, published by Harold Flammer. It is based on the seven last words of Christ.

Signs

Ministers and leaders may choose to wear black robes with or without stoles, or albs with or without stoles or chasuble.

Avoid using flowers.

Place only candles and cross in the sanctuary.

Strip the sanctuary at the end of the service. Remove all color and objects.

Leave the church stripped until the Easter Vigil.

GOOD FRIDAY

A one- to two-hour service that emphasizes the death of Christ and the human response of intercession and reflection. The service has three major sections: the Word of God, Intercessory Prayer, and Meditations on the Cross.

The service centers around a large wooden cross in a sanctuary that is still stripped. There are no flowers or paraments. Ministers and leaders wear black robes.

See *From Ashes to Fire* for an appropriate service.

1. Word of God

Follow the lectionary. Read John's Passion, John 18:1-19:42 or John 19:17-30.

Use liturgical drama or dance to act out the readings.

2. Intercessory Prayer

Follow the prayers in *From Ashes to Fire*.
Encourage free prayer by the people.
Use bidding or directed prayers.

3. Meditations on the Cross

A very powerful sign-act. After the prayers, let each person approach the cross to touch, to bow, or to kiss the cross.
Follow with prayers of confession and hope.
Leave in silence.

Hymns

BOH #412	"Ah, Holy Jesus," Heerman. Use as prayer of confession.
BOH #420	"O Love Divine, What Hast Thou Done!" Wesley.
BOH #429	" 'Tis Finished! The Messiah Dies," Wesley.
BOH #432	"What Wondrous Love Is This," American folk hymn.
SBOH #909	"I Wonder Why," Avery and Marsh. Use dramatically or with antiphonal responses.
SBOH #977	"When Jesus Wept," Billings. Use as a round or solo line.
SOZ #45	"Lead Me to Calvary," Hussey.

EASTER DAY

The most holy and joyful day of the year. Two services celebrate the central event of the Christian gospel and incorporate people into God's mighty acts of salvation: the Easter Vigil and the Second Service of Easter.
See From Ashes to Fire.

1. *Easter Vigil* or the *First Service of Easter*

This service takes place on Saturday evening (from 10:30 to 12:00 midnight) or on Sunday morning (at sunrise). The full service lasts one

Alleluia

and a half hours. This is the ideal time to baptize. It is particularly important to involve the candidates for baptism and confirmation in this service.

The service has four parts:

a. Service of Light

Gather outside.

Ignite a bonfire. Distribute candles.

Light a paschal candle (large white candle) from the bonfire and share the light with others.

Sing #401, "Christ Whose Glory Fills the Skies," Wesley.

Process into the sanctuary, which has been decorated with great banners and color. The cross has been replaced with bright religious objects and beautiful flowers such as lilies or white flowers.

b. Service of the Word

Follow the lectionary readings.

Ring bells following the readings.

c. Service of the Water

Baptize new members, especially members of the confirmation class. Use the new orders and suggestions found in the section on Baptism (Chapter V).

d. Service of the Bread and Cup

32

Use the choicest wine and bread.

Use the new orders and suggestions found in the section on the Lord's Supper (Chapter V).

Use the Easter Prayer of Great Thanksgiving found in *At the Lord's Table.*

2. *Easter Sunday* or the *Second Service of Easter*

This is the normal Sunday morning service on Easter Day. It is full of praise and joy for God's conquest over death.

Word of God

Follow the lectionary readings.

Prayers

Use only prayers of joy and thanksgiving.

Hymns

Sing the great Easter hymns.

Signs

Ministers and leaders wear albs with the most beautiful stoles or chasubles.

Celebrate baptismal renewal (Chapter V).

Banners show the *Agnus Dei* (Lamb of God).

Light a paschal candle.

Use the most beautiful white flowers, such as lilies.

Colors

Use bright, joyous colors on the best material.

H. EASTER: "JESUS CHRIST LIVES"

Easter is a season of "The Great Fifty Days" of celebration, which ends on the Day of Pentecost. *Easter* comes from the Anglo-Saxon word

Eastre, the goddess of spring. *Pentecost* comes from the Greek word *pentekoste,* which means "fiftieth."

From Ashes to Fire provides excellent resources.

Word of God

Focus on the resurrection narratives with joy and thanksgiving because Jesus Christ rose and lived on earth for forty days during this time.

Note that lessons from Acts replace the Old Testament lessons, because the church was the best witness to the resurrection. Revelation is also read to anticipate the future glory of the Lord.

On Pentecost Day, read the scripture in several languages.

Prayer

Joy and thanksgiving are the major emphases.
Avoid prayers of confession. Now is the time to rejoice.
See the *Book of Hymns,* #695ff, for Easter prayers.
See the *Book of Worship,* pp. 113ff, for prayers.

Hymns for Easter

On Easter morning use hymns of resurrection and hallelujahs.

BOH	All hymns from #437 to 452 are excellent Easter hymns. Consider reading some of these hymns as poetry.
SBOH #870	"Christ Is Alive," Wren.
SBOH #871	"Christian People, Raise Your Song," Thompson. This hymn is excellent when serving Communion on Easter.
SBOH #907	"I Serve a Risen Savior," Ackley.
SOZ #6	"Easter People, Raise Your Voices," James.
SOZ #30	"He Lives," Ackley (listed above as "I Serve a Risen Savior").
HFFW #28	"Christ the Lord Is Risen Today," Wesley and others. New tune and with many alleluias in a refrain.
HFFW #39	"I'll Shout the Name of Christ Who Lives," Vinluan.
HFFW #85	"Rise Up! All You Slaves of Evil," Wu.

For the Sundays after Easter, consider using:
SBOH #882	"Every Morning Is Easter Morning," Avery and Marsh. Use every Sunday for several weeks.

SBOH #962	"This Joyous Eastertide," Woodward. Use as an introit or call to worship.
SOZ #6	"Easter People, Raise Your Voices," James.
HFFW #1	"Behold the Man," Yuki.

Hymns for the Day of Pentecost

Use sounds like a flute trilling, wind, whisperings, sounds of Pentecost.

For confession try "If There Is a Holy Spirit," Avery and Marsh, from *Songbook for Saints and Sinners*, #65, Agape Press.

See indexes in all hymnals and supplements for hymns on the Holy Spirit.

Use creative ideas of multimedia, banners, dance, to create the kind of atmosphere of the first Pentecost. Hymn suggestions:

BOH #1	"O For a Thousand Tongues," Wesley. Use as a hymn culminating the idea of many languages on Pentecost.
SOZ #151	"I Want to Be Ready," Traditional, third stanza.
SOZ #156	"There's a Great Camp Meeting," Traditional, sixth stanza.

Special Services

See the Easter Vigil and Second Service of Easter services in Holy Week section.

Ascension Day (fortieth day of Easter or the following Sunday) is the time to declare the ascension of the Lord into heaven. Extinguish the paschal candle during the service. White is the dominant color.

Day of Pentecost is the great day of celebration. See *From Ashes to Fire* for a full service. Celebrate Communion using the Pentecost Prayer of Great Thanksgiving in *At the Lord's Table*.

The Day of Pentecost is the best time to receive new members into the church. Let this day be a celebration of receiving the confirmation candidates into the church using *A Service of Baptism, Confirmation, and Renewal*. See the section on Baptism (Chapter V) for suggestions.

Signs

Ministers and leaders wear white robes, albs, or robes with the most colorful stoles.

Light a paschal candle until Ascension Day.

Plant an Easter garden.

Use many flowers of all colors.

On the Day of Pentecost, place the baptismal font at the most prominent location; use red flowers, such as peonies; make banners with doves, flames of fire, or birthday cake; place on the table symbols of the congregation's gifts; and use red paraments, stoles, and banners.

Colors

During Easter use white or gold cloth of the finest texture for paraments, stoles, and banners.

Use red on the Day of Pentecost.

I. SEASON AFTER PENTECOST

Also called "Ordinary Time," this season begins on Trinity Sunday, the first Sunday after the Day of Pentecost, and ends with the Sunday of Christ the King, the final Sunday before Advent.

"Kingdomtide" is not a season in the ecumenical calendar. Yet the lessons often deal with the kingdom of God, God's kingdom remains a central emphasis, and United Methodists may call the Sunday that begins on the last Sunday of August "Kingdomtide" if they wish.

Word of God

Follow the lectionary.

In Year A, Matthew is read chronologically. The Old Testament lessons concentrate on the patriarchs and Moses.

In Year B, Mark is read chronologically. The Old Testament lessons concentrate on David.

In Year C, Luke is read chronologically. The Old Testament focuses on Elijah, Elisha, and the minor prophets.

The Old Testament lessons in each year will also include readings from the wisdom literature and Daniel.

Prayer

Emphasize prayers of confession, petition, thanksgiving, or intercession depending on the scripture lessons for the day. Let the prayers express the people's responses to the Word. Do not get stuck doing the same thing every week for six months.

See the *Book of Hymns*, #702ff, for prayers.

See the *Book of Worship*, pp. 126ff, for prayers.

See the collect prayers (prayers for the whole congregation to say) in the *Book of Worship* and *Seasons of the Gospel*.

Also see the collect prayers for every Sunday in *The Book of Common Prayer*.

Hymns

During Ordinary Time use your imagination to use music in different ways. Take ideas from Chapter VII (Using Hymns and Music Creatively) and use them, your own ideas, and the ideas of the congregation. But always use music that is appropriate to that particular service.

Trinity Sunday (first Sunday after Pentecost Day)

Focus on the doctrine and nature of the Trinity, but concentrate on worshiping the Trinity, not explaining the doctrine. Read (maybe antiphonally) the Athanasian Creed on Trinity Sunday.

See the *Book of Worship,* pp. 130ff, for special resources.

Use white paraments, stoles, and banners.

Sing:

BOH #344	"Come Father, Son, and Holy Ghost," Wesley.
BOH #26	"Holy, Holy, Holy," Heber.
BOH #463	"We Believe in One True God," Clausnitzer.

The Sundays after Pentecost are the best time for the occasional services of the church year such as preaching missions, the Wesleyan services, and other special services. (See Chapter VI.)

These Sundays present the best opportunity to begin a more frequent (weekly, biweekly, monthly) celebration of the Lord's Supper. But the Communion days should be set by the church calendar, not the secular calendar.

All Saints' Day (first Sunday in November)

See suggestions in *From Hope to Joy*.
An autumn festival that remembers the whole paschal mystery of death
and resurrection. A good service to remember the saints of a local church.
All Saints' Day may also take the place of a local homecoming.
Use the lessons for All Saints' Day from *Seasons of the Gospel*.
Let the people call out or read names of saints.
Remember congregational, denominational, and ecumenical saints.
Put the names of saints on banners, stations, and bulletins.
Display pictures of saints.
Baptize on this day.
Celebrate Communion using the All Saints' Great Thanksgiving from
At the Lord's Table.
Use the best vestments.
Light many candles.
Display the best flowers available.
Use red or white paraments, stoles, and banners.
Some suggestions for hymns:

BOH #534	"For the Might of Thine Arms," Horne.
BOH #536	"For All the Saints," How.
SOZ #63	"What Are They Doing in Heaven?" Tindley.
SOZ #195	"God's Amazing Grace," Martin.
HFFW #21	"The Grace of God Unbounded Is," Tsiang, stanza four.
HFFW #36	"For the Bread Which You Have Broken," Benson, stanzas two and three. (See BOH #314 with a different tune.)
HFFW #82	"Once to Every Man and Nation," Lowell, stanza three. (See BOH #242 with a different tune.)

Thanksgiving Day

See suggestions in *From Hope to Joy*.
See hymn indexes for many hymns of thanksgiving.

Sunday of Christ the King (last Sunday after Pentecost)

See suggestions in *From Hope to Joy*.
Use white paraments, stoles, and banners.

Signs

Ministers and leaders may wear various robes, albs, or other clothing, with or without stoles.

The worship space and contents each week should correspond to the Word and the human response.

See Chapter X on Environment.

Colors

Let the colors and textures of paraments, stoles, and banners reflect the Word of God. For example, a Sunday reading that demands repentance should be accented with purple colors. On a Sunday with a joyful reading, use white colors. Vary the colors and textures each week.

IV. WE GATHER TOGETHER: THE BASIC SERVICES

Each service of worship takes its cue from the season in which it occurs. Then, remembering to be biblical, simple, and balanced, plan the service with an internal consistency that allows the Word of God to speak clearly to human life and for people to respond to the Word. The four-part pattern of *We Gather Together*—Entrance and Praise, Proclamation and Praise, Responses and Offerings, and Sending Forth—provides the best available pattern for the typical United Methodist services. Other worship patterns, which are at times also acceptable, are also used by United Methodist churches. But whatever service pattern is used, the hope is that *We Gather Together* will so guide the devotional life of all United Methodists that hearing and responding to the Word of God becomes the basic dynamic of Christian life.

A. PLANNING WORSHIP SERVICES: THE ESSENTIAL STEPS

There are several steps in planning every service of worship. They should be used by all leaders of worship—ministers, musicians, choir directors, singers, ushers, readers, acolytes, altar guild members, worship committee members, and Communion stewards—who plan together.

1. *Study the Word of God: The Foundation*

a. Study all three scripture lessons for the day and their relationship to the season of the church year. *Seasons of the Gospel* lists these readings. Richard Eslinger's *Introducing the New Common Lectionary* (Worship Alive Series) lists all the readings and psalms of the new lectionary.

b. Study the Psalm for the day. Find the Psalms in *Seasons of the Gospel.* The Psalm gives guidance to congregational responses to the Word. See the *Book of Hymns,* (index #847) or *Psalms for Singing* for Psalms that may be sung.

c. Write a simple sentence declaring the major emphasis of the scripture lessons.

2. *Determine the Human Response: Our Reply*

a. Discuss the human reality to be emphasized in light of the scripture and psalm. Ask, "How do I respond to this Word?" or "How does my congregation respond to this Word?" or "Where does the Word hurt?" or "Where does the Word help?"

b. Identify the collect prayer for the day. The collect helps set the theme of the human response. *See Seasons of the Gospel,* the *Book of Worship,* pp. 66ff, the *Book of Hymns,* #676ff, *The Book of Common Prayer,* and H. T. Allen's *A Handbook for the Lectionary* (Philadelphia: Geneva Press, 1980) for additional collects for each day of the church year.

c. Choose the hymns for the day. See the United Methodist Planning Calendar for suggestions. See the indexes to the *Book of Hymns, Songs of Zion,* and *Supplement to the Book of Hymns* for songs that correspond to the readings. The congregation may also have indigenous hymns and music that may be appropriate. See Music in Worship (Chapter VII) for suggestions on how to introduce new music and how to use music creatively.

d. Write a simple sentence declaring the major emphasis of the congregation's response to the Word.

3. Plan the Pattern of Worship

a. The preferable pattern of worship is that of *We Gather Together* that uses resources from the *Supplemental Worship Resources* series.

Be aware that this is only a pattern to give order and coherence to worship, not a formal ritual to be followed absolutely.

This basic pattern is Entrance and Praise, Proclamation and Praise, Response and Offering, and Sending Forth.

b. Other patterns may also be appropriate, depending on the scripture and human response. Always let the form of worship follow the function of worship. The pattern of Adoration, Confession, Thanksgiving, Intercession, Offering, Narration, and Sending Out may be used. Or the service may use a pattern of Worship, Teach, Proclaim, and Serve. Or the service may use the pattern of a Revival, Love Feast, Watchnight Service, or other special service.

See G. T. Sparkman's *Writing Your Own Worship Materials* (Valley Forge, PA: Judson, 1980) for other suggestions of worship outlines.

4. Prepare the Sermon: The Link Between the Word and Human Life.

a. Use *Preaching the New Common Lectionary,* the *Proclamation* series, *Knox Preaching Guides, Interpretation* series, and *Preaching the Liturgical Year* to help develop approaches to sermons.

See also the *Abingdon Preacher's Library* (Nashville: Abingdon) for some excellent resources.

b. Write a simple sentence declaring how the sermon bridges the gap between the major emphasis of the scripture and the central response by the congregation.

5. Plan the Actions of the Service

Let the actions be appropriate to the Word and response. See Movement in Worship (Chapter IX).

6. Plan the Environment of Worship

Let all sights and smells aid the service. See Environment of Worship (Chapter X).

B. MUSIC

The Word and Table pattern of worship in *We Gather Together* offers excellent opportunities for the placement of music in creative and appropriate places. It rejects the "slot theory" of placement of music that involves using the hymns and anthems in the same place each week. Instead, leaders of worship should look at the flow and movement of each service: what follows, what illumines, what carries out the theme, what interprets, and what "fits best." Examples and suggestions in the following sections may be used as listed and will stimulate your own imagination in the creation of new approaches.

1. *Entrance and Praise*

Gathering

The congregation may sing the prelude and the "old hymns" which they love.

Use instruments as either solos or ensemble preludes.

Ask the organist to use a certain hymn as a prelude to teach a new hymn for use later in the service.

Use this time of gathering to teach a new hymn, new response, psalm antiphon, or to give information about special music for the day.

Use the musical prelude to set the tone for the service:

Expectant and mystical for Advent,

Joyful throughout Christmas and Epiphany,

Somber for Lent,

Alleluias throughout Easter,

Wind and mystery followed by joyful in Pentecost,

Various moods during Ordinary Time.

Following the music and gathering, do not say, "Now let us worship." As people gathered, the worship began as appropriate "work of the people."

Greeting

The way in which leaders greet the people often sets the total mood of the service. If leaders greet with enthusiasm, confidence, and strength, they strengthen the total service.

The choir or congregation can sing scripture readings as the greeting. For example, use one of Paul's greetings to the early churches.

Use antiphonal singing between the choir and the congregation, using hymns of greeting. Example:

BOH #77, "Come Christians Join to Sing," Bateman.
Let the choir sing the lines, followed by the congregation responding with alleluias.
All sing the third line.

Use a solo voice singing the greeting, sometimes from the balcony or another place in the sanctuary.
Use the choir singing the greeting as they stand in the aisle rather than processing immediately to the choir loft.
Let the total congregation sing just a refrain of a hymn or short stanza for the greeting. Use it for several weeks. The congregation will then memorize and remember it. Example:

BOH #233: "Rejoice, Rejoice, Give Thanks and Sing," Wesley. Use refrain only.

Use some of the new settings of psalm antiphons (*alive now!*, "Singing Our Prayers," July/August 1981; "Holy Festival," July/August 1983; and *Psalms for Singing*—all available from The Upper Room, 1908 Grand Avenue, Nashville, TN 37202). Use each setting for several Sundays so that the antiphons become familiar. Examples of other hymns which can be used as greetings:

BOH #5	"Come Ye That Love the Lord," Watts.
SBOH #929	"Morning Has Broken," Farjeon.
SOZ #2	"Glory Be to Our God on High," James, stanza two.
SOZ #218	"Let the Heav'n Light Shine on Me," Carter.
CEL II #8	"O Look and Wonder, How Good It Is," Lockwood.
CEL II #19	"O Come, Let Us Sing a Hymn to You," Achón.
HFFW #61	"Come, O Come to Me," Nagasaka.

Hymn of Praise

It is most appropriate that the first hymn be one of praise and thanksgiving to God.
The hymn should be familiar.
The hymn should be strong.
The hymn should be sung with enthusiasm and not too slowly; it

should not drag. The organist may play staccato to help lead the congregation.

The hymn may be one from a wide variety of hymns, depending upon the context of the service and the liturgical season.

The entrance hymn of praise may be a theme hymn during certain seasons. (See suggestions for creative use of hymns.)

A choir and the other leaders of worship may process to the front of the sanctuary during this hymn, carrying banners, the Bibles, candles, the cross, etc. Do not try to keep in a march step. Walk naturally.

A suggestion: Have each family unit put a bell on a ribbon and give that bell to the church. Then all bells are to be attached to a processional board and used each Sunday morning. The bells give a lovely tinkling sound—the music of the families of the church. This procession of the bells should be finished before the hymn of praise begins.

It is appropriate to stand for the hymn of praise.

Sometimes use the processional hymn for all people to enter the sanctuary at the same time for a special type of service, especially on Palm/Passion Sunday.

Eliminate "amens" on hymns of praise.

Opening Prayers

Responses to the opening prayer are quite appropriate, with the congregation singing a refrain or a hymn response.

Sing one special hymn or refrain throughout a liturgical season.

The United Methodist resources have tremendous prayer hymns. Use them as congregational hymns, solos, readings by the pastor, antiphonal songs, anthems by the choir, and for silent reading as the organist plays the melody. Find the hymn which fits your service, lectionary, theme, and needs of your congregation. The richness and depth of the hymn will reach many hearts. Examples of refrains:

BOH #311	"We Beseech Thee, Hear Us," Pollock.	
BOH #119	"O Lamb of God, I Come," Elliott.	
BOH #469	"Thy Kingdom Come, O Lord," Housman.	
SBOH #874	"I Will Arise and Go to Jesus," Hart.	
SBOH #864	"Because He lives," Gaither.	
CEL II #24	"May the Words of My Mouth," Psalm 19:14.	
SOZ #67	"I Surrender All," Van De Venter.	

Many hymns can be spoken or sung as a prayer. Examples of prayer hymns:

BOH #272	"Lead, Kindly Light," Newman.
BOH #273	"God, Who Touches the Earth with Beauty," Edgar.
BOH #170	"O Master, Let Me Walk with Thee," Gladden.
SBOH #191	"Just a Closer Walk with Thee," Traditional.
SOZ #165	"Give Me Jesus," Traditional.
SOZ #83	"Sometimes I Feel Like a Motherless Child," Traditional.
CEL II #27	"Samba of Confession," taken from scripture.
HFFW #2	"Give Us, O God, the Grace to See," Kronmann.

Act of Praise

This is a good place for an anthem of praise, often an anthem based on a psalm. The text of the anthem, however, should dictate whether it would be appropriate here. Sometimes the anthem would best come between the scripture lessons, following the sermon, as the benediction, or in another place.

If the psalm from the lectionary is read, the psalm is often read during this act of praise. The congregation may respond more naturally and with more enthusiasm to the psalm with antiphon rather than responsive readings. (See Singing the Psalms in Chapter VII.) Suggestions for acts of praise:

Use the traditional doxology or other doxologies, BOH #809-812 and SOZ #246. Try using the traditional doxology words of Thomas Ken to the tune BOH #19, Lasst Uns Erfreuen, using the alleluias. Caution: Be sure to print the words of the doxology in the bulletin because it is difficult to remember them when using another tune.

Use BOH #493, the last stanza of which is the doxology, as a round. A new group can enter at the beginning of any measure. Be sure to give good instructions and directions when teaching. Sing this stanza in rounds for several weeks so the people become familiar with it.

Use a hymn either read or sung as a litany that fits the lectionary and theme of the day appropriately.

2. Proclamation and Praise

Prayer for Illumination

This prayer can either be spoken or sung. The prayer asks for guidance as we hear both the words of scripture and the words of the preacher as the Word is proclaimed. *Suggestions* of hymns which can be sung by the congregation, solo, choir:

BOH #267   "Open My Ears," Scott (second stanza).
BOH #369   "Break Thou the Bread of Life," Lathbury (first stanza). (Sing second stanza after the reading of the scripture.)
BOH #372   "O Word of God Incarnate," How.
SBOH #956 "Spirit of the Living God," Iverson.
SOZ #245   "Hungry and Thirsty, Lord, We Come," Smith.
CEL II #15   "The Word of the Lord," translated by Deschner.
CEL II #24   "May the Words of My Mouth," Psalm 19:14.
HFFW #49   "Send Your Word," Imakoma.

Scripture

Many anthems and solos are set to the exact words of scripture. Sing these scripture lessons instead of, or as a supplement to, the reading of the scripture.

Many hymns are based on scripture. (See "Index of Scripture References, Canticles, and Other Aids to Worship," BOH #846, and the Index for HFFW.) Use these hymns following the reading of the scripture with perhaps a few words of transition and explanation of the hymn's use of the scripture. For interpretation see:

Companion to the Hymnal, Gealy, Lovelace and Young (Abingdon Press, 1970)
Companion to The Book of Hymns Supplement, H. Myron Braun (Nashville: Discipleship Resources, 1982)
The Gospel in Hymns, Albert Bailey (Charles Scribner's Sons, 1950)

If a psalm is appropriate, sing the psalm using an antiphon, a hymn based on that psalm, or a choral setting of the psalm of which there are many. (See index to *Celebremos II* and the section on Singing the Psalms.)

Acclamations may be sung after the scripture is read. There are many "alleluias" which can be sung following the reading of the scripture; also refrains from hymns. Examples:

BOH #19   "Alleluia" from "Ye Watchers and Ye Holy Ones," Riley.
BOH #66   "Alleluia" from "Praise, My Soul the King of Heaven," Lyte.
BOH #505   "Jubilate, Amen" from "Now, on Land and Sea Descending," Longfellow.
BOH #536   "Alleluia" from "For All the Saints," How.
SOZ #98   "Glory, Glory, Hallelujah," Traditional (stanza three).
CEL II #17   "Alleluia" from "Alleluia," Psalm 19.
CEL II #9   "Alleluia" from "Heaven Is Joyfully Singing," Suppe and Achón.
HFFW#32   "Hallelujah" from "Hallelujah, Christ Is Risen," Feliciano.

Sermon

The "Word" event is too important to have it be only a "word" event. Use music and the arts to help communicate the message of the gospel.

Use a hymn as the sermon theme, or as the thought pattern of the sermon.

Quote the words of a hymn in the sermon.

Base a whole series on one idea. Example: Preach on the theme of the cross, using a different hymn about the cross on each Sunday.

Close the sermon with a hymn, and then have the congregation *immediately* stand and sing that hymn.

Tell the story of the writing of a hymn as the major part of a sermon.

Use musical presentations to "tell the story" at the time of the sermon.

Have the word danced or interpreted by members of the church or community.

Divide a hymn into its stanzas that present different ideas. Have the congregation sing one stanza, then preach on the meaning of that stanza—followed by all stanzas in the same form.

49

3. Responses and Offerings

Prayer

Use a hymn as a prayer for confession and pardon. Examples:

BOH #115   "Dear Master, in Whose Life I See," Hunter (repentance).

BOH #254   "How Happy Every Child of Grace," Wesley (forgiveness).

SBOH #944   "O the Lamb," Campmeeting (pardon).

CEL II #23 "Lord, Have Mercy Upon Us," Suppe (petition).

HFFW #56   "Oh, the Eyes of Christ the Lord," Umeda (repentance).

Use a hymn or refrain as an invitation to prayer. Examples:

BOH #257   "Blessed Jesus at Thy Word," Clausnitzer.

BOH #262   "Talk with Us, Lord," Wesley. Use different stanzas.

BOH #802   "Lead Me, Lord," Psalms 5:8, 4:8.

BOH #803   "Listen to Our Prayer," text from India. Use solo voice or choir unaccompanied.

SBOH #890   "Give Me a Clean Heart," Douroux.

SOZ #70   "A Prayer for Love," Lincoln.

SOZ #232   "Prayer Call and Response," Wesley.

HFFW #14   "O Come, Creator Spirit," Fortunatus.

Use a hymn as a litany of prayer, including caring needs of the congregation. Examples:

BOH #542   "This Is My Song," Stone and Harkness.

SBOH #956   "Spirit of the Living God," Iverson.

SBOH #878   "Dear Lord, for All in Pain," Carmichael.

BOH #235   "Dear Lord and Father of Mankind," Whittier.

SOZ #95   "I Want Jesus to Walk with Me," Traditional.

SOZ #123   "There Is a Balm in Gilead," Traditional.

Use a hymn or refrain following the prayer. Examples:

BOH #119   "Just As I Am" Elliott (the refrain, "O Lamb of God I
            Come, I Come").
BOH #470   "God of Grace and God of Glory" Fosdick (the
            refrain, "Grant us wisdom, grant us courage").
SBOH #942   "Our Father," Matthew 6:9-13.
SOZ #248   "Agnus Dei."
SOZ #249   "The Lord's Prayer."
CEL II #23 "Lord, Have Mercy Upon Us," Suppe.

The Offering

The offering is a symbolic offering to God of ourselves and all that we have. This is a time when instrumental music can be given as a gift to God and to the congregation. There are no words to concentrate on, but the music can speak to the heart.

If only one anthem is sung on a Sunday morning, it should not be placed as an offertory anthem. People are busy with passing the plates and other distractions and cannot listen to the text chosen with care for that Sunday. If a choir sings a second anthem, however, it may be sung at this time.

Congregational singing can be used during the offering time, or following the offering. Examples:

BOH #181   "We Give Thee But Thine Own," How.
BOH #525   "For All the Blessings of the Year," Hutchinson.
BOH #523   "O Lord of Heaven and Earth and Sea," Words-
            worth (stanza five).
SBOH #970   "What Gift Can We Bring," Marshall.
SBOH #877   "We Give Thanks" ("Demos Gracias al Señor"),
            translated by Frances.
SOZ #228   "Thank You, Lord," Traditional.
SOZ #229   "We Give Thee What We Have, Lord," Hobbs.
SOZ #231   "God Is So Good," Anonymous.

Doxologies

Traditional words by Thomas Ken, BOH #809, the Great Doxology, can be sung to #19 BOH.

BOH #493	Tune to Tallis Canon, sung in round (stanza five).
SOZ #230	Elaborate accompaniment to familiar tune.
SOZ #238	"Doxology" (with festive air).
SOZ #246	"Doxology" (different tune).

Other Responses

There is an unlimited number of ways to use music as a response to the Word:

Use a hymn as a response to what has been preached, summing up ideas of the scripture and sermon.

Use an anthem to respond to the lectionary and the sermon.

Use quiet music from an organ or other instrument for meditation and commitment. *Example:* "Blessed Quietness," SOZ #206, Ferguson.

Use a hymn as a commitment hymn to be sung by the people. Examples:

BOH #105	"God Calling Yet! Shall I Not Hear," Terstegen.
BOH #435	"When I Survey the Wondrous Cross," Watts.
SBOH #874	"Come, Ye Sinners, Poor and Needy," Hart.
SBOH #919	"Just a Closer Walk with Thee," Traditional.
SOZ #29	"I Know Who Holds Tomorrow," Stanphill.
CEL II #41	"Yes, My Lord," Mellado.
HFFW #77	"Living with the Lord," Lee.

Use a hymn as an affirmation of faith. Examples:

BOH #89	"Thou Hidden Source of Calm Repose," Wesley.
SBOH #885	"Faith, While Trees Are Still," Frostenson.
SBOH #887	"Father, I Adore You," Coelho.
SOZ #11 and	
SBOH #884	"Father, I Stretch My Hands to Thee," Wesley. Follow with the Apostles' Creed.
HFFW #3	"God Created Heaven and Earth," Traditional.

Baptism (See Chapter V.)

The Lord's Supper (See Chapter V.)

52

4. *Sending Forth*

Because the congregation should be the choir, let the congregation sing the final benediction. See indexes in the supplemental books and hymnals for benedictions. Examples:

BOH #236	"Savior, Again to Thy Dear Name," Ellerton.
BOH #306	"Blest Be the Tie That Binds," Fawcett.
BOH #342	"Go Make of All Disciples," Adkins.
BOH #539	"God Be with You Till We Meet Again," Rankin.
SBOH #893	"Go In Peace," Koenig.
SBOH #894	"Go Now in Peace," Sleeth (round).
SBOH #948	"Peace I Leave You," Traditional.
SOZ #203	"God Be with You," Dorsey.
SOZ #250	"Benediction" with narration, Smith.
CEL II #46	"Worship Has Ended" (with alleluias), Gomes.

Use a variety of alleluias from hymns. (See section above on responses to scripture reading.)

C. OTHER SUGGESTIONS

These are a few suggestions about each phase of a service of worship. The outline follows the pattern suggested by *We Gather Together*.

1. *Entrance and Praise*

Let the announcements come first. Only announce meetings or issues that involve the whole congregation. Be brief. During this time, introduce the congregation to new songs, music, responses, actions, or movements that will be used during the service.

The Gathering may be a time of silence and meditation, or a joyful time to greet old and new friends.

The Greeting, or Call to Worship, which speaks to the people, establishes the theme of the service. Responsive readings that are brief and poetic are best.

The Invocation, spoken to God, thanks God for the opportunity to worship.

See *Writing Your Own Worship Materials* and the *Monthly Misselette* (J. S. Paluch, 1800 W. Winnemac Avenue, Chicago, Illinois 60640) for some good ideas about these introductory offerings.

Also see Heth Corl's *Lectionary Worship Aids A,B,C* (Lima, Ohio: C.S.S., 1978) for some good helps.

See the opening sentences in the *Book of Hymns*, #773ff, and in the *Book of Worship*, pp. 66ff.

Choose an uplifting hymn that is familiar to the people as the first hymn.

This is not the correct place for creeds or offerings.

Use psalms of praise.

2. *Proclamation and Praise*

Scripture Readings

Let a large Bible be open, visible, and used.

Begin with a prayer specifically for the Word read, preached, and heard, such as a Prayer for Illumination.

Place Bibles in each pew rack. Or use bulletin inserts to print the lessons for each week.

Before the scripture readings, sing from the *Book of Hymns*, #795-8.

Use lay readers.

Introduce each lesson with several short introductory sentences.

Invite the congregation to read along with the reader. The *Book of Hymns,* #620ff, has several scripture passages that the congregation may read, or pew Bibles may be used.

Read all three lessons, even if they are not used for the sermon.

Use the whole scripture lessons, not abbreviated texts.

Let the congregation stand for the Gospel lesson.

After each lesson, let there be a collect prayer, hymnic antiphon, or a psalm read or sung.

Psalms

Let psalms be responses to the scripture lessons.

Do not let the psalms substitute for the Old Testament lesson.

See Singing the Psalms in Chapter VII.

Sermon

a. Steps in Sermon Preparation

(1.) Study the texts by doing solid exegesis.
Use commentaries.
Compare translations.
Understand the text in its context.
Study the literary form.
Learn the historical situation.
Do word study.
Finally, state the purpose of each lesson in the Christian context and explain the central burden of the text in one simple sentence, in one simple image, or as one simple story.
(2.) Ask concrete questions.
What is the issue in the context?
Where is that issue real in contemporary settings?
What is the answer provided by the text?
Where is that answer applicable in a real-life setting?
Finally, state the human reality addressed by the passage in one simple sentence.

b. The Sermon in Worship

Preach from the whole lessons, not just a few words from an isolated text.

Re-read or retell the scripture lesson as a part of the sermon.

Be clear about the specific intent of the sermon and how it should touch persons' lives: to teach the mind, or to delight the emotions and heart, or to move the affections and will.

Keep the sermon short, sharp, and clear.

Fifteen to eighteen minutes is the best length for a sermon.

The best sermon images are Bible stories, your own personal stories, and the stories of others. See Storytelling (Chapter VIII).

3. *Responses and Offerings*

The Wesleyan tradition strongly encourages a varied response to God's living Word. Leaders of worship must offer the people several possible ways to reply to God's Word besides going to the altar for church membership or public confession, or going home to think about the sermon.

Prayer

Always address prayer to God, not to the people.

Rules for all prayer: stress verbs, avoid adverbs and adjectives, make sentences short and simple, and strive for rhythm and rhyme.

Avoid pastoral prayers that are too long or too vague. When a pastoral prayer is offered, keep it short: less than three minutes or three hundred words. Use the prayer to lift specific pastoral concerns to the Lord.

Receive prayer requests.

Let the "collect" prayer guide the structure of other prayers: name of God, attribute of God, petition, consequence of petition, and doxology.

Use bidding or directed prayers with moments of silence. These prayers are the best for involving a whole congregation in prayer.

Encourage lay persons to lead prayer.

Use silent prayer. Not all prayers need to be verbal displays.

Encourage corporate confession, corporate intercession, corporate petition, and corporate thanksgiving.

Vary formal and free prayer.

Use hymns as prayers, either spoken or sung.

Other Responses

Invite people to share their needs, concerns, and celebrations publicly.

Provide quiet time for reflection. Let each pew become a prayer rail. Let people raise their hands, sign cards, or stand to respond.

Invite people to come to the communion rail to pray.

Recite creeds.

Receive an offering. Receive not only offerings of money but also letters to public officials, date books, commitment cards, or pieces of paper with special concerns.

Offertory prayers may either precede or follow the offering. These prayers focus on the gifts, the givers, and the giving.

Sing songs that respond to the Word. See Music in Worship (Chapter VII).

Invite people to be baptized or to renew their baptismal covenant. See Baptism (Chapter V).

Receive the Lord's Supper. This is typically the most appropriate response to the Word. See the Lord's Supper (Chapter V).

Let movement aid responses. Have people kneel, pass the peace, or use the "orans" position (head erect or lifted, arms out at side and flexed, palms forward). Use liturgical dance to respond, or liturgical drama. See Movement (Chapter IX).

4. *Sending Forth*

The Benediction or Dismissal sums up the whole service, and sends forth the people into the world with power.

This is a blessing by God on the people. The benediction/blessing may be signalled by a hand action. Holding your hand in one of several ways, move your hand down from head level to waist level, then to chest, then from left shoulder to right shoulder.

Invite the congregation to participate in singing the Amen(s).

Vary the choral Amens. See the *Book of Hymns, #816-825.*

See the hymns for "Going Forth from Worship" in *A Supplement to the Book of Hymns, #883, 893, 894, 928, 935, 948.*

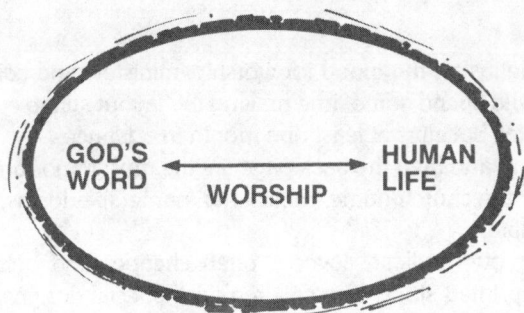

See the Amens in *A Supplement to the Book of Hymns, #860, 893, 939, 942.*

Final Comments

Inclusive language

Sermons, prayers, and other original work should not use language that excludes people due to sex, age, race, or culture. Scripture may be altered when the intent of the text is to be inclusive.

Acceptable changes might be from man/men/mankind to people, all people, women and men, humanity, persons, everyone, all of us, all, folk, kin, and we; from sons of God to people of God, children of God, God's people, daughters and sons of God; from brothers to sisters and brothers, kindred, and family.

See "The Use of Inclusive Language in the Worship of the Church," available from Bookstore, Wesley Theological Seminary, Washington, D.C. 20016.

Transitions

Watch the transitions in worship. Does the service move clearly and smoothly from each part of the service to the next? Is there intentional progress in the service?

The Sunday Bulletin

See D. A. Wiltse's *Designing the Sunday Bulletin* (Worship Alive series, available from Discipleship Resources).

a. Preparation

Because bulletins set the mood for worship, ministers and concerned lay people should spend some time making the layout suitable.

Make plans for bulletins at least one month in advance.

The front page and then the back page are the most important pages. Always include the church name, minister(s)' name(s), address, phone, location, and date.

Making your own bulletin cover is often cheaper and better than purchasing preprinted stock. Use children's art, special designs, or pictures of local highlights such as stained glass windows or steeples.

Use artwork to enhance, not clutter the bulletin.

b. The Service Itself

Mark clearly each instance of congregational participation, especially where to stand or where to sit.

Avoid large empty spaces.

Major headings such as Entrance and Praise should not interrupt the flow of the service.

Insert the words of anthems, and names of authors and composers.

c. Reproduction

Of various kinds of equipment available for producing the bulletin, offset presses offer the best quality and the most flexibility. But they are expensive, may be messy, and require great skill.

Copiers are most convenient and versatile. Yet the machines are not as durable and the cost per page is the highest among all methods.

Mimeograph machines, when used with electric stencil cutters, are the least expensive. The copies are not of as high quality but can produce adequate copies.

d. Use

Mail out bulletins weekly. Bulletins mailed weekly have a larger readership than monthly newsletters.

For further help with bulletins and graphics, see:

Logos Art Productions, Inc.
346 Chester Street
St. Paul, Minnesota 55107

Center for Communications Ministry
1962 S. Shenandoah
Los Angeles, California 90034

V. THE SACRAMENTS

The sacraments of Baptism and the Lord's Supper are the primary responses of people to the Word of God. Each signifies, in its unique way, the most intimate interaction between God and people. The sacraments should always follow the Word read and preached, and be the highlight of the service. They have always been central to the Wesleyan tradition and must today regain their prominence.

See Ole E. Borgen's *John Wesley on the Sacraments* (Nashville: Abingdon, 1972) for the best theological insights into Wesley's sacramental theology.

A. BAPTISM

Baptism, in the tradition of John Wesley, washes away original sin, brings people into covenant with God, admits people into the church, turns children of wrath into children of God, and makes people heirs of God's kingdom. It is central in Christian life and must be so in worship.

Baptism should always be a festive occasion.

See L. H. Stookey's *Baptism, Christ's Act in the Church* (Nashville: Abingdon, 1982) and W. Willimon's *Remember Who You Are* (The Upper Room, 1980).

To train the people regarding baptism, use the multimedia kit, *Baptism* (Nashville: Graded Press, 1978).

Preach on baptism at least once yearly.

Use *A Service of Baptism, Confirmation, and Renewal* as found in *We Gather Together.*

Pastoral Comments

Baptize particularly on the Day of the Baptism of our Lord, Easter Day, Pentecost Day, and All Saints' Day.

Nonverbally, walk through the whole service to be certain that actions correspond to what is said.

Baptize on Sunday morning before the whole congregation.

Let the baptismal font or pool be continually in view of the congregation. This is also true on Sundays without baptisms.

Preach on baptism prior to the sacrament and center the whole service on the sacrament.

Let the water be visible: pour the water from a clear glass pitcher from a height into the font or pool.

Offer thanksgiving over the water.

Thoroughly wet the baptized person by dipping infants or using immersion or pouring.

Encourage the congregation to watch the baptism; do not block their view. Ask the parents, family, or sponsors to stand to the side of the minister.

Seal the candidate with oil, using a pure oil and marking the candidate's forehead with the sign of the cross.

Put new clothes on the initiate. A baptismal bib or gown may be made by the congregation.

Light a baptismal candle.

In the covenant renewal service, sprinkle the people with water thrown by an evergreen branch, or invite the people to come and touch the baptismal water, or invite the people to come to the Communion rail to pray. (See below for the specific service of baptismal renewal.)

Ministers should strictly observe the Wesleyan tradition that forbids ministers to rebaptize people. The theological and pastoral problems are too great to allow the practice. Yet if a person wishes to publicly demonstrate a new relationship with God, encourage the person to renew her or his baptismal covenant. Use *A Service of Baptism, Confirmation, and Renewal* for this practice, and follow this pattern:

A Service of Baptismal Reaffirmation

Introduction (no changes).

Presentation: The minister says: "I present *[name(s)]* for the renewal of the baptismal covenant." Then the candidate(s) come forward.

Renunication of Sin and Profession of Faith (no changes).

Thanksgiving over the Water (no changes).

Renewal of the Baptismal Covenant: Addressing the candidate(s), the minister says: "Remember your baptism and be thankful."

The candidate(s) may then touch the water and then touch their forehead, or kiss the water, or just touch the water, or kneel at the baptismal font/pool.

Then the minister lays hands on the candidate(s)' head(s) and says: "*[Name(s)]*, the power of the Holy Spirit work within you, that, having been born through water and the Spirit, you may continue to be a faithful witness of Jesus Christ."

Commendation and Welcome (no changes).

Confirmation

Confirmation prepares older youth and adults to assume the full responsibilities of Christian discipleship. It should be a rigorous time of spiritual growth, which enables the candidates to be formed in faithful Christian living. To make confirmation a full period of preparation:

1. Begin the confirmation training with a service of dedication of the candidates on the First Sunday of Advent. You may use Wesley's "Covenant Renewal Service."

2. Ask the candidates weekly to read the lectionary lessons (or the lessons for the next Sunday), from the First Sunday of Advent to the Day of Pentecost. Study the lessons each week with the class.

3. Ask the catechumenates to give one-half hour a day to study of the Word and to prayer.

4. Pray for the candidates by name each Sunday, from the First Sunday of Advent to the Day of Pentecost.

5. Encourage the catechumenates to help lead in each service of

worship, especially by reading the scripture lessons and leading the prayers. Use the candidates in all the special services of the two great cycles of the church year. Suggestions are given in each earlier discussion of the seasons of the church year.

6. Ask the candidates to tithe of their income during the six-month period.

7. Ask the candidates to give one hour a week in service to other people during the six-month period.

This whole pattern, if followed, will emphasize the virtues and responsibilities of Christian living, as well as cognitive knowledge. See the new confirmation material for junior highs from Cokesbury, "Journey into Faith," to help develop this pattern.

Hymns

There are several spots in the service of baptism where it is appropriate for the congregation to sing a stanza of a hymn or a baptism hymn. Some suggestions:

1. The minister says, "We believe in the church, and we believe that Jesus Christ is the foundation of this church, whose creation is the water and the Word." The congregation then sings stanzas one and two of BOH #297, "The Church's One Foundation," by Stone.

2. When the water is poured into the font, the congregation sings about water; stanzas three and four of BOH #126 "Jesus, Lover of My Soul," by Wesley.

3. At the end of the service, the closing words are those of fellowship and community of the church united in Christ. A fitting hymn would be BOH #193, "Jesus, United by Thy Grace," stanzas one, two, three, and others if time permits.

The best baptismal hymns are found in the *Supplement to the Book of Hymns*. If the whole congregation does not have access to the *Supplement*, the choir or soloist may sing one or more of these:

SBOH #856 "All Who Believe and Are Baptized," Kingo.
SBOH #879 "Descend, O Spirit, Purging Flame," Brenner.
SBOH #923 "Like Survivors of the Flood," Avery and Marsh.
SBOH #946 "Praise and Thanksgiving Be to God," Yardley and Whiteley.
SBOH #902 "Have You Got Good Religion," Traditional.

Following is a suggested list of hymns from the *Book of Hymns* that might be used in the *Service of Baptism* (1964) or in *A Service of Baptism, Confirmation, and Renewal* (alternate service, 1976), of The United Methodist Church. The list is compiled by Roger Deschner, and edited by Bonnie Jones.

God's Saving Acts in the Presence of Water

Creation
#480   "Thou, Whose Almighty Word," Marriott (Alternate tune: Italian Hymn)

Deluge
#125   "Jesus, Lover of My Soul," Wesley, stanzas 1 and 2
#147   "If on a Quiet Sea," Toplady

Exodus   (Suitable for baptism at Easter)
#446   "Come, Ye Faithful Raise the Strain," John of Damascus

The Idea of Washing (Cleansing and Forgiveness)

#93   "Come Thou Font," Robinson, stanza 1
#125   "Jesus Lover of My Soul," Wesley, stanzas 3 and 4
#293   "Glorious Things of Thee Are Spoken," Newton, stanza 2
#421   "There Is a Fountain," Cowper, stanza 2

The Idea of Death and Resurrection

#441   "Now the Green Blade Riseth," Crum
#442   "Spring Has Now Unwrapped the Flowers," Oxford Book of Carols
#454   "Hail, Thou Once Despised Jesus," Bakewell

Initiation into the Faith

96   "I Sought the Lord," Anonymous
#128   "O Happy Day," Doddridge, stanzas 1 and 2 before, and then 3-5 after the baptism

Advent Hymns

#354	"O Come, O Come, Emmanuel," Latin—12th century
#355	"Lord Christ, When First Thou Cam'st," Bowie
#360	"Come, Thou Long-Expected Jesus," Wesley

Entrance into the Church (Fellowship with the Saints, the Royal Priesthood)

#193	"Jesus, United by Thy Grace," Wesley
#297	"The Church's One Foundation," Stone
#301	"All Praise to Our Redeeming Lord," Wesley
#530	"Christ, From Whom All Blessings Flow," Wesley
#535	"Happy the Souls to Jesus Joined," Wesley
#536	"For All the Saints," How

New Relationships with Jesus Christ, Union with Him

# 48	"How Firm a Foundation," Rippon (note "deep waters" in stanza 3)
# 84	"O Guide to Every Child," Clement of Alexandria (a very early Christian hymn)
# 86	"Shepherd of Eager Youth," Clement of Alexandria (different translation of #84)
#312	"See Israel's Gentle Shepherd Stand," Doddridge (only baptism hymn listed as such)
#418	"O Sacred Head Now Wounded," Trans. Gerhardt
#432	"What Wondrous Love Is This," American folk hymn
#507-8	"Come Let Us Use the Grace Divine," Wesley (covenant)

Regeneration: New Creature

#283	"Love Divine, All Loves Excelling," Wesley
#342	"Go Make of All Disciples," Adkins (stanza 2)
#344	"Come, Father, Son, and Holy Ghost," Wesley
#464	"See How Great a Flame Aspires," Wesley (note blessing of *rain*)

Baptism Conveying the Holy Spirit: Illumination, Enlightenment

# 29	"O Splendor of God's Glory Bright," Ambrose of Milan
#131	"Come, Holy Ghost, Our Hearts Inspire," Wesley (idea of anointing)
#135	"Holy Spirit, Truth Divine," Longfellow
#132	"Holy Ghost, Dispel Our Sadness," Gerhardt
#403	"Walk in the Light," Barton
#462	"Spirit of Life, in This New Dawn," Marlatt
#466	"Come Down, O Love Divine," Bianco Da Siena
#467	"Come, Holy Ghost, Our Souls Inspire," Rhabanus Maurus

Hymns for Confirmation

#86	"Shepherd of Eager Youth," Clement of Alexandria
#155	"He Who Would Valiant Be," Bunyan (consider the sexist words)
#170	"O Master, Let Me Walk with Thee," Gladden
#185	"More Love to Thee, O Christ," Prentiss
#240-1	"Fight the Good Fight," Monsell
#246	"My Soul Be on Thy Guard," Heath
#268	"O for a Closer Walk with God," Cowper
#467	"Come, Holy Ghost, Our Souls Inspire," Rhabanus Maurus
#478	"Lead On, O King Eternal," Shurtleff

Roger Deschner also suggests:

#238	"Christian, Dost Thou See Them," Andrew of Crete (an early Christian hymn)
#249	"Awake, My Soul, Stretch Every Nerve," Doddridge
#250	"Soldiers of Christ Arise," Wesley

Hymns for Renewal

#133	"Breathe on Me Breath of God," Hatch
#134	"Come Holy Spirit, Heavenly Dove," Watts
#135	"Holy Spirit, Truth Divine," Longfellow
#136	"O Spirit of the Living God," Tweedy
#139	"Author of Faith, Eternal Word," Wesley

#180	"Awake, My Soul, and with the Sun," Ken (stanza 2)
#182	"Lord, in the Strength of Grace," Wesley
#187	"Take My Life and Let It Be Consecrated," Havergal
#470	"God of Grace and God of Glory on Thy People Pour Thy Power," Fosdick

B. THE LORD'S SUPPER

The Lord's Supper, in the tradition of John Wesley, is the primary response to the Word of God. According to Wesley, the Holy Meal was not only a memorial service but was also a sure means of grace in which Jesus Christ was present, a stimulus to future hope, and a sacrifice by Christ for humanity and by people for God. Because of the rich meaning of the meal, Wesley received the Lord's Supper, on average, every two days throughout his entire life. United Methodists must recover the richness of Wesley's sacramental theology and practice.

To train the congregation, use the multimedia kit, *Holy Communion* (Nashville: Graded Press, 1978).

Use *The Sacrament of the Lord's Supper* as found in *We Gather Together*. Study the new pattern by using *Word and Table*. Supplement your practice of Communion by using *At the Lord's Table,* a collection of Prayers of Great Thanksgiving.

Also, ministers should study Melissa Kay's *It Is Your Own Mystery* (Washington: Liturgical Conference, 1977) for useful suggestions on serving the Lord's Supper.

Pastoral Comments

Serve more frequently: biweekly or monthly. Especially celebrate Communion in relation to the church year: the first Sunday of Advent, Christmas Eve or Day, the Day of Epiphany, the first Sunday of Lent, Palm/Passion Sunday, Easter Vigil, Day of Easter, Day of Pentecost, All Saints' Day.

Colors should be those of the season, not exclusively white. This is true of paraments, stoles, and banners.

Pull the altar or Communion table away from the back wall or use a free-standing table.

Clear the table or Communion table of all clutter such as flowers or candlesticks.

Remove barriers between the people and table.

The ministers may wear a chasuble (poncho-like garment) over the alb (white robe with full sleeves).

Encourage a member of the congregation to bake the bread and then bring the bread to the table with the offering. See R. Eslinger's *The Bread We Bake* (Worship Alive Series, available from Discipleship Resources) for bread recipes.

Use a large chalice (cup).

Stand behind the table, facing the people.

Use orans position for prayer (head erect or lifted, arms out at side and flexed, palms forward).

Encourage the people to stand through the prayer of Great Thanksgiving, and then sit to say the Lord's Prayer.

Let all the actions be visible: *take, bless, break, give.*

Use the appropriate Prayer of Great Thanksgiving. *At the Lord's Table* provides twenty-two prayers plus other suggestions for Communion.

Sing the Sursum Corda and Sanctus. See the *Book of Hymns,* #836 and #843.

Pray the Prayer of Great Thanksgiving with intensity.

Let the ushers be gentle guides, aiding the congregation to the table.

Styles of Distribution

1. Communion services in Advent, Lent, and other times of penitence (such as at a revival), demand a style of distribution that encourages people to kneel and to be humble in the presence of God. Each of the following styles enables people to be more reflective as they receive and meditate upon the Lord's Supper. On these days, while the people move quietly during the distribution, the choir may sing anthems.

a. Ministers and lay servers stand in front of the Communion rail. People form a single line, come one by one to the servers, kneel (or stand), receive the elements, and then either proceed to the Communion rail to kneel and pray, returning to their seats when they wish—or return immediately to their seats after receiving, for a time of prayer and meditation. This style of distribution takes the least amount of time of these three methods.

b. Ministers and lay servers stand in pairs behind the Communion rail. Individuals, when they desire, come to the Communion rail and kneel. A pair of servers immediately provides the elements. Individuals may then remain for silent prayer as long as they wish, and then return to their seats. When one person leaves the rail, another takes the place, and the pattern is repeated. This style requires a longer time for distribution.

c. Ministers and servers stand behind the Communion rail. People come by tables (small groups), kneel together; all receive the elements at the same time, hear a blessing, rise, and return to their seats. Then another table comes forward. This style takes the longest time of any method of distribution.

2. Communion services in Christmas, Easter, and other joyful times (such as All Saints' Day), demand a style of distribution that encourages the mingling and free movement of people. Each of the following styles enables people to rejoice in the Lord's Supper, and take a relatively short time to distribute. The whole congregation may sing hymns during the distribution on these days.

a. Ministers and servers stand at the table, divide the elements, and place them on trays. Servers then pass the trays from person to person, pew to pew, each person serving the one seated next to him or her. This method takes the least amount of time.

b. Ministers and servers divide into pairs and stand at several places in the worship area. People then come, stand, and receive from the servers closest to them. People then return to their seats. This method takes a longer time.

c. Ministers and servers stand at one place at the front of the sanctuary. People form a single line, come, stand, receive, and return to their seats. This method takes the most time of these three methods.

Some options to personalize the service of Communion are to make eye contact, call out the person's name, or touch his or her hand.

Sing during the distribution, led by choir or song leader. Use lively and joyous music to avoid being too penitential.

End with a time for silent prayer: about three minutes seems best.

The best practice for all leaders of worship is to walk through the whole service nonverbally and see if all actions are consistent, helpful, and reflect the appropriate meaning.

Ministers should strictly avoid "drop-in" Communion services. These services deny the basic reality that the Holy Meal is a community act that joins the people and God.

Hymns

The leaders of worship might want to teach the congregation the full Communion service, with chanting, in the back of the BOH (#830), although the mood of that service is more penitential and confessional than the new alternative service. Teach the people to chant, using the instructions for chanting at BOH #662. Sing all responses.

The Lutheran Church, Missouri Synod, has developed some very joyful music to be used with the new interpretation of the Eucharist as a joyous feast. This music can be adapted to "We Gather Together," an alternate service.

The choice of whether the congregation sings during the serving of the sacraments is a decision to be made by the minister and the worship committee. If you do sing hymns, be sure to choose enough so you do not run out of hymns before everyone receives. Suggestions:

BOH #326
and # 327   "Here, O My Lord, I See Thee Face to Face," Bonar. Use first three stanzas before or while receiving, stanzas 4 and 5 after receiving.
BOH #324   "Let All Mortal Flesh Keep Silence," St. James. Give background to the Liturgy of St. James and the age of this text.

70

BOH #328	"How Happy Are Thy Servants, Lord," Charles Wesley
BOH #332	"O the Depth of Love Divine," Wesley. Charles Wesley wrote many hymns for the Lord's Supper. Recover these from the BOH and other sources of Wesley materials.
SBOH #865	"Become to Us the Living Bread," Drury. Sing during the service.
SBOH #932	"Now Let Us from This Table Rise," Kaan. Sing following communing.
SBOH #912	"In Remembrance," Courtney. Sing just before the service as an anthem or congregation. Instruct congregation about the repeats and the ending.
SBOH #957	"Take Our Bread," Wise. Sing as the sacraments are brought forward during the offering.
SBOH	See the index for many other excellent Communion hymns.
SOZ #243-250	Communion Music for the Protestant Church
CEL II #14	"Song for Communion," Gabaraín
CEL II #29	"Christ Lives," Arias
HFFW #30	"Do You Know Me?" Chen.
HFFW #36	"For the Bread Which You Have Broken," Benson (#314 BOH with different tune).

VI. OCCASIONAL SERVICES

These services celebrate particular times in the lives of individuals and congregations.

A. WEDDINGS

Services of high celebration that should always worship God and form people in their faith.

See *Planning a Christian Wedding,* by L. H. Weems (Worship Alive Series, available from Discipleship Resources).

Use *A Service of Christian Marriage* in *We Gather Together.*

See P. H. Biddle's *Abingdon Marriage Manual* (Nashville: Abingdon, 1974) for some helpful comments and useful services.

Formation of the Congregation's Ministry

Be clear about who is responsible for what. Develop a church checklist or handbook for duties.

Teach about weddings and marriage in workshops, talks, sermons, and during pre-marital counseling.

Preparation

The couple and minister together are in charge.

Be clear that the service reflects the faith of the couple.

Christian weddings should be limited to Christian couples.

Wedding directors, musicians, florists, and photographers will want to help influence the shape and flow of the wedding, yet the minister and couple have the final responsibility.

The Wedding

Encourage photographs before the service rather than after, to allow the wedding party immediately to participate in the reception.

1. Entrance and Praise

Music precedes the service by fifteen minutes. Be clear that the music is Christian.

The best time for special songs.

Be creative in joining the wedding party. The father does not always need to give away the bride.

2. Proclamation and Praise

Let the friends and family share thoughts and gifts with the couple.
Let the couple share gifts with each other and the congregation.
Sing psalms.
Use scripture and avoid secular poems.
Sermons should be short and addressed to the couple and congregation. The sermon may be based on the lectionary readings for the day or a topic chosen by minister and couple.

3. The Marriage

The vows should reflect the faith of the couple.

4. Thanksgiving

Various responses may include: passing of the peace, hymns, psalms, sharing by the congregation, the Lord's Supper, or a Love Feast.

5. Sending Forth

Sums up the whole service.

Signs and Colors

White colors and signs dominate the setting.
Avoid the excessive use of flowers.

After the Wedding

Provide a full copy of the wedding service to the couple.
Work hard at integrating the couple into the congregation.
Remember anniversaries during congregational worship.
Encourage couples to renew vows during worship services or on anniversaries. See the ritual for marriage renewals in *A Service of Christian Marriage.*

Hymns

The wedding is a worship service. Therefore, it is very appropriate for the congregation to sing hymns, especially during the processional and the recessional. Suggestions:

BOH # 38   "Joyful, Joyful We Adore Thee," Van Dyke
BOH # 49   "Now Thank We All Our God," Rinkart

BOH # 66	"Praise My Soul, the King of Heaven," Lyte
BOH # 67	"The King of Love My Shepherd Is," Baker on 23rd Psalm
BOH # 55	"Praise to the Lord, the Almighty," Neander
BOH #283	"Love Divine, All Loves Excelling," Wesley
BOH #329	"Jesus, Thou Joy of Loving Hearts," Attributed to Bernard of Clairvaux
BOH #375	"Love Came Down at Christmas," Rosetti. Use if it is a Christmas wedding.

It would be wise for the worship committee of the church to have a policy about the use of popular music during the wedding ceremony and during the prelude and gathering time. It is highly recommended that popular music not be used during the prelude, service, or postlude, but be confined to the reception. A written policy can guide the couple in deciding these matters.

See *A Repertoire List of Music* (Worship Alive Series, available from Discipleship Resources), for additional suggestions of music for weddings. Also write to the Section on Worship, Board of Discipleship, for other appropriate hymns and sources of hymns and music for weddings.

B. FUNERALS

Funerals are services of worship, not only memorials for the deceased, and both reflect and form faithful life. In general, United Methodist funerals need much improvement in their conduct and in the role they play in the whole worship life of a congregation.

See *A Service of Death and Resurrection* (Nashville: Abingdon, 1979) and L. H. Weems, *Planning a Christian Funeral* (Worship Alive Series, available from Discipleship Resources).

Use *A Service of Death and Resurrection* in *We Gather Together*.

See P. H. Biddle's *Abingdon Funeral Manual* (Nashville: Abingdon, 1978) for some helpful comments and useful services.

Formation of the Congregation's Ministry

Teach about dying, death, funerals, and grief before death.

Preach about death and life, particularly at Easter, homecomings, and All Saints' Day.

Be clear about the congregation's responsibilities.

Help people prepare their own funerals by helping them choose music, hymns, scripture, and other requests.

Preparation

Pray with and for the dying. See *Ritual in a New Day* and *The Book of Common Prayer* for services with the dying and their families.

Plan funerals with the dying and their families.

Ministers and family have the final responsibility for funeral plans.

The Funeral

1. Entrance and Praise

The service should be held in the local church sanctuary.

Limit the use of flowers.

Cover the casket or urn with a funeral pall. The pall is a large, beautiful cloth, bearing the symbol of the cross.

An excellent time to hold the funeral is in the evening, the night before the burial. Let this "wake" time, when many friends and family are present, be the time for the service.

2. Proclamation and Praise

The time to read favorite scripture lessons of the deceased.

Proclaim the whole paschal mystery of death and life.

Acknowledge and affirm those who are living.

Acknowledge grief and hope.

Do not replay the whole of a person's life.

See W. A. Poovey's *Planning a Christian Funeral* (Minneapolis: Augsburg, 1978) for some useful ideas about funerals and some excellent illustrations of funeral sermons.

3. Offering of Life

Pray together the Lord's Prayer.

Sing hymns of celebration and comfort.

Sing Easter hymns.
Encourage others to remember the deceased.
Celebrate Communion.

4. Sending Forth

Reflects the whole service.

5. Committal

Fraternal services, if any, should be held before the final committal. While some pastors prefer to have the committal prior to the fraternal rites, all such actions should be in the total context of a worship service.

Some ministers prefer to have committals prior to the funeral, making God the center of the service rather than the body of the deceased.

Signs and Colors

White colors and signs dominate the setting.

Avoid the excessive use of flowers, and see that they do not cover up religious objects.

After the Funeral

Provide a full copy of the service to the family.

Reintegrate the mourners into the congregation at worship. Ask other members who have grieved to visit those who mourn.

Remember the dead by name at Easter, homecoming, All Saints' Day, Charge Conference, special memorial services, and on the anniversaries of death.

Hymns

It is quite appropriate for the congregation to sing hymns as part of the worship service. Hymns of praise and thanksgiving are appropriate, as are hymns of comfort and hope. Favorite hymns of the family should be considered. Use hymns sung by congregation, choir, or soloist. Use hymns quoted in funeral sermons. Use the texts as poetry in the service. Suggestions:

BOH # 9   "I'll Praise My Maker While I've Breath, Watts. This hymn was sung by John Wesley as he died.

BOH # 20   "A Mighty Fortress Is Our God," Luther

BOH # 28   "O God Our Help in Ages Past," Watts

BOH # 47	"God of Our Life," Kerr
BOH # 48	"How Firm a Foundation," Traditional
BOH # 51	"Give to the Winds Thy Fears," Gerhardt
BOH # 56	"Through All the Changing Scenes of Life," Tate and Brady
BOH # 67	"The King of Love My Shepherd Is," Psalm 23
BOH # 68	"The Lord's My Shepherd, I'll Not Want," Scottish Psalter
BOH #234	"O Love That Wilt Not Let Me Go," Matheson
BOH #290	"I Know Not What the Future Hath," Whittier. Consider another CM tune more familiar such as Armenia.
BOH #302	"Come Let Us Join Our Friends Above," Wesley
BOH #445	"I Know That My Redeemer Lives," Medley
BOH #450	"Thine Is the Glory," Budry
BOH #535	"Happy the Souls to Jesus Join," Wesley
BOH #259	"Jesus, Thy Boundless Love to Me," Gerhardt
BOH #530	"Christ, From Whom All Blessings Flow," Wesley
BOH #536	"For All the Saints," How
BOH #289	"Abide with Me," Lyte
BOH #291	"On Jordan's Stormy Banks I Stand," Stennett
BOH #288	"Servant of God, Well Done," Wesley
BOH #440	"Sing with All the Songs of Glory," Irons
SBOH #878	"Dear Lord, for All in Pain," Carmichael
SBOH #936	"O Jesus Christ, to You May Hymns," Webster
SBOH #919	"Just a Closer Walk with Thee," Traditional
SBOH #921	"Kum Ba Yah," Traditional
SBOH #922	"Lift High the Cross," Kitchin and Newbolt
SBOH #956	"Spirit of the Living God," Iverson
SOZ #7	"Close to Thee," Crosby
SOZ #28	"Farther Along," Stevens
SOZ #38	"No, Not One!" Oatman, Jr.
SOZ #41	"Stand by Me," Tindley
SOZ #95	"I Want Jesus to Walk with Me," Traditional
SOZ #123	"Balm in Gilead," Traditional (chorus only)
SOZ #139	"Kum Ba Yah," Traditional
CEL II #5	"My Shepherd Is the Lord," Psalm 23
CEL II #6	"God Is My Rock," Psalm 62
CEL II #25	"Give Us Your Light," Lockwood
CEL II #31	"We Have Hope," Pagura
HFFW #2	"Give Us, O God, the Grace to See," Kronmann
HFFW #52	"The Sun Is Rising O'er the World," Sambika
HFFW #61	"Come, O Come to Me," Nagasaka

C. REVIVALS AND PREACHING MISSIONS

Revivals and preaching missions are to convert sinners, to renew the faith of believers and whole congregations, and to sanctify those people seeking perfection. Typically, the services are now for the present members of the church and should be structured so as to enhance faith.

Prepare Oneself

Each leader of worship should determine if and why there is a need for special services. Be clear about personal and congregational goals.

Prepare the Congregation

Involve as many people as possible as early as possible.

The people should set the agenda. Let the evangelism or preaching committee meet with the preacher to alert the preacher to the congregation's needs.

Let the people do the advertising, publicity, special arrangements, and major leadership of worship.

Encourage Bible study by individuals and groups to prepare the people for the services. Acts and Ephesians have suitable texts.

Plan several occasions for the people to meet with the preacher, both before and after the services.

Involve children, youth, and adults of all ages in each aspect of the work.

Worship Services

Use models that focus on song, prayer, sermon, and responses.

Sing the old favorite hymns. Tell the stories of the old hymns.

Use the services to teach new hymns that convey the spirit of the moment.

Let choirs sing, but do not let choirs replace congregational song.

Prayer should be extemporaneous, yet short and sharp.

The sermon may be longer than normal, but clarity and focus are essential.

Employ various congregational responses to the preached Word of God: standing, coming forward to the altar rail, signing cards, kneeling at the pew, silent prayer, or raised arm.

End all services with a good hymn and people holding hands in a circle around the sanctuary.

Conclude the series of services with a special service of thanksgiving such as a Love Feast (below, Chapter VI), or Communion (Chapter V), or a Covenant Renewal Service (Chapter V).

D. WESLEYAN SERVICES

These services are a unique part of the Wesleyan tradition, particularly emphasizing responses to the Word of God read and preached. Their recovery will greatly aid in the renewal of worship.

Love Feast

A joyous, free service that focuses on fellowship, song, prayer, and testimony. Through the nineteenth century, the love feast was the single most popular of all Methodist services.

See Frank Baker's *Methodism and the Love Feast* (London: Epworth, 1964).

Use Hoyt Hickman's *How to Hold a Love Feast* (Discipleship Resources).

Study the Love Feast service in the *Book of Worship*, p. 389.

Use quarterly, especially at Thanksgiving.

Church suppers are good occasions for these services.

Fellowship halls are excellent locations for Love Feasts.

Serve love feast loaves and hot tea, coffee, or chocolate.

Local bakers love to bake love feast loaves. One recipe:

1 cup hot, dry, mashed potatoes, unseasoned
½ cup scalded milk
1 cup sugar
½ cup butter
2 eggs beaten
1 ½ pounds of flour for soft dough
¼ tsp. nutmeg
2 pkgs. yeast
½ cup warm water
2 tbsp. orange rind
2 tbsp. orange juice
½ tsp. mace

Cream butter and sugar together. Add mashed potatoes, mixing well. Add lukewarm milk, eggs, mixing well. Dissolve yeast in warm water and add to mixture. Combine seasonings, flavorings, and rinds, and add to mixture. Stir thoroughly. Add 2 ½ cups flour and mix. Add enough more flour to make a soft dough. Knead on well-floured table. Form into a ball and place in a greased bowl. Cover with a clean cloth and let rise in warm place until double in size. Punch down and let rise again for 5-10 minutes. Flouring hands well (the dough will be very sticky), form into small balls of about three ounces. Place on a cookie sheet. Slash top with razor blade to release air, cover, and let rise until doubled in size. Bake in 350° oven until golden brown all over (about 15-20 minutes).

Hymns

Hymns can be chosen according to the category needed: praise, fellowship, thanksgiving. See indexes.

It would be appropriate and interesting to use only Charles Wesley hymns in a Love Feast, since it is a unique part of the Wesleyan tradition. Suggestions:

Praise:	BOH #1	"O For a Thousand Tongues to Sing"
	BOH #15	"Praise the Lord Who Reigns Above"
Fellowship:	BOH #301	"All Praise to Our Redeeming Lord"
	BOH #310	"Jesus, We Look to Thee"
Thanksgiving:	BOH #341	"Jesus, the Name High Over All"
	BOH #409	"Ye Servants of God"

Watch Night Service

An excellent service to end the old year and begin the new year. The service was popular in colonial Methodism and emphasizes song, prayer, preaching, and testimony.

See the *Book of Worship*, pp. 382ff, for one pattern. But use whatever pattern seems to be most appropriate to the local situation.

Combine with a Covenant Renewal Service.

Covenant Renewal Service

A good service when the congregation and/or individuals wish to renew baptismal and membership vows. This service has historically been very popular in British Methodism.

This service properly replaces rebaptism.

Use on the last night of the old year, the first day or first Sunday of the new year, or on the Day of Epiphany.

See the *Book of Worship*, pp. 382ff, for one service.

A service in this tradition may use the pattern of *A Service of Baptism, Confirmation, and Renewal* (Chapter V).

United Methodist Heritage Celebrations

These resources may be appropriate as United Methodists celebrate their history:

Jubilee (Cokesbury) describes "We Belong to a Singing People." This provides an excellent study and service of Wesleyan hymnody.

Words from the Wesleys (J. Marshall, Agape: Illinois) is a set of three choir anthems that set the words of John Wesley to some beautiful music.

We Go Forward! Stories of United Methodist Pathmakers (C. and L. Wolcott, Discipleship Resources, 1984) provides stories that may be told during worship.

Bicentennial Moments (R. L. Hunt, The Upper Room, 1983) offers brief sketches of United Methodist history that may be read during worship.

E. OTHER SPECIAL SERVICES

There are many unique services that punctuate the ordinary worship life of a congregation. They should be used to emphasize special events and spiritual needs, and as such they add variety to liturgical life. Listed below are resources for these services.

Ritual in a New Day

This book contains ideas and resources for a service of footwashing on Maundy Thursday and other days, a service of naming for an adopted child, a service with the dying, a service with the divorced (controversial yet insightful), and a service for beginning and ending a ministry (for use at the onset or conclusion of a pastoral appointment).

Book of Worship (Methodist Publishing House, 1944)

This first book of worship by the former Methodist Church contains many unique and interesting services, such as a rite with the sick.

Book of Worship (1964)

This official book of worship for United Methodists contains eighteen special services including consecrations, installations, recognitions, institutional services, and dedications. It is a rich resource of practical services. Now see *Blessings and Consecrations* for a contemporary update of these services.

Resources from other communions

- *The Book of Worship* (Minneapolis: Augsburg, 1978), the Lutheran Book of Worship
- *The Book of Common Prayer* (Seabury Press, 1979), the Episcopal Book of Worship
- *The Book of Common Prayer* (Oxford: Oxford University Press, 1968), the Church of England Book of Worship
- *The Alternate Service Book* (Oxford: Oxford University Press, 1980)

Each of these service books is useful to supplement and enrich our own United Methodist resources.

Morning Prayer Service and Evening Prayer Service

These services are excellent for pastors, other leaders of worship, and small church groups. They form the basic pattern of daily devotion.

See *alive now!* (Nashville: Upper Room, July/August 1983) for two beautiful services that are useful for United Methodists.

See *Praise God in Song* (Chicago, IL: GIA) for other daily services.

See *A Guide to Prayer for Ministers and Other Servants* (Nashville: The Upper Room).

Thanksgiving for Birth or Adoption of a Child

See the *Book of Common Prayer,* pp. 439ff, and *A Service of Thanksgiving for the Birth or Adoption of a Child* (Princeton: Consultation on Church Union).

Services of Healing

See Frank Stanger's *God's Healing Community* (Nashville: Abingdon, 1982) for the theology and practice of these powerful services.

See the *Book of Common Prayer,* pp. 453ff, for "Ministration to the Sick."

See *Blessed to Be a Blessing,* James K. Wagner (The Upper Room, 1983) for a working model of a healing ministry with seven services of worship.

Services of Reconciliation

To help heal divisions between people and groups. See the *Book of Common Prayer,* pp. 447ff, for "A Service of Penitence and Reconciliation."

VII. MUSIC IN WORSHIP

WHY WE USE MUSIC IN WORSHIP

United Methodists have a heritage of being a singing people. It is vitally important to continue and expand that heritage. This can be accomplished through liturgy, which means "the work of the people." This "work" includes music. Through music in the liturgy, the people . . .

- *Praise* God;
- *Respond* to God and the divine revelation as found in the scriptures;
- Express their deep *emotional* feelings;
- *Verbalize* their faith;
- *Learn* and express theology;
- Experience *community;*
- Feel the *mystery* of life;
- Fulfill the *biblical mandates* of the Psalms, Paul, and others to "Sing Unto the Lord";
- Experience music as *pastoral care* in healing, sustaining, guiding, and reconciling words and feelings;
- Make new *commitments* or renew old commitments to Christ as Lord;
- *Hear the Word* afresh and new.

BASIC PRINCIPLES OF MUSIC IN WORSHIP

Good congregational singing and music in the church are the responsibility of everyone.

Do not take congregational singing for granted. It takes time, effort, and plans to help the congregation sing well.

The pastor, choir director, organist, and other leaders of worship should know thoroughly and use broadly the music resources of The United Methodist Church: BOH, SBOH, SOZ, CEL II, and HFFW. The supplements enrich and update our musical heritage since the *Book of Hymns* was published in 1966.

The leaders of worship should plan worship three months in advance. Preview lectionary readings well in advance if preaching from the lectionary. The choir director needs the scripture and the theme of the service several weeks in advance to choose appropriate music and prepare it with the choir.

Pastor and musicians must work closely together in planning worship and in understanding worship and liturgy.

Be pragmatic when planning music in worship. Use what is available to you through your resources and the talents of your people.

Be aware of new musical repertoire and new ideas for the use of music in worship. Do not stagnate: "But we've always done it this way!"

Do simple things well.

A. TAKE A HYMN SURVEY

One of the most important pieces of information any pastor or musician should have is the nature of the congregation's repertoire. What are the hymns the congregation knows and likes to sing? You can get that information several ways:

1. In your hymnal or in a notebook, keep a record of the hymns that are sung. Do this each week.

2. Go back through several years of old bulletins and make a list of hymns that have been used.

3. Ask some active members of the church to mark your hymnal with the hymns the congregation loves and sings.

Perhaps the best way to get this information is through a hymn survey. This can be done easily by preparing a list of about fifty hymns. (Most churches have a repertoire of 40-60 hymns.) Ask for the following information on a survey sheet:

• Age group.
• Denominational background. (This makes a great deal of difference.)
• List the fifty hymns taken from the survey of the last ten years of bulletins.
• Have a place where the congregation can mark that the hymn is:
  Fairly familiar
  Very familiar
  Very meaningful
  (Instruct respondents to leave blank those hymns which they do not recognize or know.)

Tally all the information. This survey provides information about a congregation's hymnological tastes: what the people know and like to sing.

After you have this survey information you can add to the repertoire four or five new hymns a year. (See Section D of this chapter on Introducing New Hymns.) Give variety and breadth to the hymn repertoire.

(See *The Hymn,* published by The Hymn Society of America. Wittenburg, University, Springfield, Ohio 45501, and an article, "Managing the Congregation's Hymn Program—How to Proceed," July 1981, p. 147, written by Dale Ramsey.)

B. MAKING THE CONGREGATION A CHOIR

Because liturgy is "the work of the people," the people must do their work and not have others do it for them. Too often most of the music has been left to the choir, which has been thought of as a performing group. But great congregational singing can and should happen.

Several principles are involved in this concept of the congregation as choir. (See *Congregation as Choir,* in Worship Alive Series available from Discipleship Resources.)

1. If the people are to do their work in liturgy they must be allowed to sing hymns which are meaningful, familiar, and helpful to them.

2. The major responsibility of the choir is to lead the congregation in singing.

3. Choirs often need to learn new music. So, too, the congregations need to learn something new when it is needed and appropriate. (See Section D of this chapter, Introducing New Hymns.)

4. Let the congregation sing in fellowship suppers, Sunday schools, smaller groups. Encourage much singing in the church.

C. SELECTING HYMNS FOR WORSHIP

It is best to use at least three hymns during the service: a hymn of praise, a hymn either preparing for the Word or responding to it, and a hymn of sending forth.

1. The opening hymn of praise should be familiar to the congregation.

2. Do not sing more than one unfamiliar hymn in any one service. Teach it to the congregation before the service.

3. If you have sung a new hymn, repeat it on following Sundays so the congregation may become familiar with it.

4. Read through the hymn to make sure that the theology of the text is appropriate for the scripture and sermon of that particular worship service.

Do not just use the "slot theory" of placing hymns where they have always been. Think through the flow and movement of the service. Where does the hymn fit most appropriately and helpfully? Example: Do not use a hymn such as "Go Make of All Disciples" as your opening hymn. (See Music in We Gather Together, Chapter IV.)

Consider the repertoire and ability of your congregation.

Tell the congregation why a new hymn is being chosen.

Keep a record of the hymns sung, either in a personal hymnal or in the office in a notebook.

Use a personal hymnal as a workbook with notes on hymns, history of hymns, use with scripture, when the hymn was sung, and other pertinent information.

Theology varies greatly from hymn to hymn. Be aware of the differences. Example: From the hymn "Beneath the Cross of Jesus" come the words, "Content to let the world go by." Contrast that with "Soldiers of Christ Arise."

It is not always necessary to sing all stanzas of a hymn. Read through the hymn, however, to understand the flow of the poetry. If there is a stanza that does not fit, leave it out and note in the bulletin the verses to be sung.

Use a hymn that responds to or illumines a sermon series. Use it throughout the sermon series.

Use a familiar tune to new words, if that text is appropriate but the tune is too difficult or too unfamiliar to the congregation. (See Section F of this chapter, Using the Metrical Index.)

D. INTRODUCING NEW HYMNS

Introducing new hymns is a continual process of education and encouragement. But the benefits are great. It encourages a variety of the use of hymns and broadens vision and understanding. There are ways to introduce new hymns successfully.

1. Use Wesley's "Comments on Singing," p. viii in *Book of Hymns,* as a challenge to better singing.

2. One of the most important aspects is to tell the congregation *why* a new hymn has been selected.

3. Provide firm vocal and instrumental leadership.

4. Pastor and musicians must be enthusiastic and communicate anticipation to the congregation.

5. Have the organist play the hymn as part of the prelude so the people begin to hear the new melody.

6. Teach the hymn to the congregation for about five minutes at the beginning of the service during the gathering. Plan these five minutes well.

- Tell briefly why the hymn has been chosen for that Sunday.
- Explain any words which are new or difficult.
- Have the choir sing through one stanza.
- Have the congregation sing through the stanza at least twice.
- Compliment members of the congregation on how well they sang.
- Another possibility: Line out the hymn, line by line, and have the congregation learn it line by line.

7. Write bulletin notes giving the background of the hymn and the story of who wrote it, when, and why. (Use *Companion to the Book of Hymns, Companion to The Book of Hymns Supplement, The Gospel in Hymns,* and other resources listed in the Musical Bibliography.)

8. Use a "Hymn of the Month" occasionally, perhaps during Advent or Lent, or for a special series.

9. Teach the "Hymn of the Month" by using children's choirs, fellowship suppers, instrumental groups, special organ arrangements, anthem arrangements, or following #6 above.

10. If you teach a new hymn, sing it again soon so that the congregation becomes familiar with it and it becomes a friend.

11. Use visual aids to teach a new hymn. (See *22 Ways to Teach a Song,* Choristers Guild, 2834 W. Kingsley Road, Garland, Texas 75041.)

E. USING HYMNS AND MUSIC CREATIVELY

Creativity means putting together something old in your mind with something new. We can all be creative if we are willing to risk the new "product" of creative thinking.

This is one way to make the Word and the story of God's gift in Christ new and fresh and alive to people who have heard the story over and over again.

There are many ways to use hymns in fresh and creative ways. Many of these ideas are incorporated in the suggestions throughout this chapter and for the various seasons. This list includes some of those ideas, but is just a beginning to get your imagination started. Take the list, use it, and apply it—for reform and renewal of music!

1. Let sermons grow out of thought patterns and ideas of a hymn.
2. Build a series of sermons around a group of hymns that develop a theological subject.
3. Use hymns as calls to worship, sometimes read antiphonally.
4. Use hymns as prayer responses.
5. Use hymns as scripture preludes and responses.
6. Use hymns as responsive readings.
7. Use hymns as a litany with the needs of the community and the world spoken between stanzas.
8. Use hymns as prayers (sung or read) by the minister alone or with the congregation.
9. List the hymns in the bulletin for use as meditations before the start of the service.
10. Illustrate hymns with slides of famous paintings, nature scenes, or other subjects.
11. Develop a hymn festival using a theological theme, historical sequence, hymns of one writer, or liturgical year.
12. Tell the background of a hymn before singing it. Print "Hymn Notes" in the bulletin.
13. Give the history of hymnody and how a particular hymn fits into it.
14. Use a "Hymn of the Month" periodically to teach new hymns.
15. Use antiphonal singing of hymns in various combinations: men alternating with women, or choir with congregation, or right side of the chancel with left.
16. Use antiphonal singing when the hymn has questions and answers. Example: "What Child Is This?" BOH #385.
17. List the hymn writer and composer of the tune in the bulletin each Sunday to familiarize the congregation with important names in hymnody.

18. Use hymns on appropriate Sundays of the church year. Example: Advent hymns for Advent.

19. Use dance or movement to interpret a hymn.

20. Dramatize the words of the hymn.

21. Make a banner that interprets the hymn with color design and key words.

22. Use familiar words to new tunes. People begin to think about the words in a new way. (See Section F of this chapter, Using the Metrical Index.)

23. Use new words to familiar tunes. (See Section F of this chapter, Using the Metrical Index.)

24. Use words of a hymn to close the sermon and then have the congregation immediately stand and sing that hymn. Repetition is a powerful teacher.

25. Use the organ alone on a stanza while the congregation reads the text either together aloud or silently.

26. Use "Concertatos"—anthem settings of familiar hymns, where the choir sings the more difficult parts and the congregation joins in on part of the anthem.

27. Use a hymn as the theme for special liturgical seasons. (See Advent and Lent.)

28. Use hymns for your personal daily devotions. The hymnal is a treasure store of religious poetry and 3,000 years of salvation history.

29. Have a special study on "How to Use the Hymnal."

30. Use your hymnal as a workbook. Make notes on the pages of the dates when hymns were used. Make notes on alternate tunes. Make notes on scripture passages.

31. "Good music" exists when certain music is good for certain people on a certain day. Use a variety of hymns to make sure that the music is "good" for each day.

32. Use a wide variety of hymns. Every style has its own contribution to make to the many needs of the congregation.

33. Use the "Gathering" for learning new hymns. This is part of worship and the "work of the people."

34. Use a solo or anthem in place of the reading of the scripture if the words of the text are the same.

35. Use antiphons to let the congregation respond to the reading to the Psalms. (See below, Singing the Psalms.)

36. Divide the stanzas of a hymn according to what they say. (See example for the Lord's Supper.)

37. On some Sundays let the people sing the prelude as they are

gathering rather than an instrumental prelude. Give them an opportunity to sing some of their favorites.

38. Choose hymns which interpret and illumine the scripture which was read. (See BOH Index #847: Index of Scripture References of Hymns.)

39. Encourage hymn memorization by the congregation by using repeated refrains or hymns.

40. Use cassette recordings for aged and shut-in members.

41. Have a lending library of hymn recordings.

42. Have a section of the church library reserved for books on hymns and hymnals. Highlight these in the bulletin.

43. Encourage hymnals in the home, and hymn singing by families.

44. Integrate hymns and church school curriculum. Probably no hymn is too difficult for children to learn. They love to know the stories behind the writing of the hymn and the history of it.

45. Let children introduce a new hymn to the congregation.

46. Sponsor a hymn writing contest.

47. Sponsor a hymn-playing class to teach members of the congregation to learn to play hymns.

48. Choose hymns carefully for funerals and for weddings. These are worship services and the hymns and music should be appropriate for worship.

49. Use instrumental groups to play unfamiliar hymn tunes to help acquaint the congregation with these new tunes.

50. Become familiar with the hymns, supplements, and other helps for the creative use of music and other arts in worship.

Alleluia

F. USING THE METRICAL INDEX
(#850 in the *Book of Hymns*)

The metrical index is probably the most mysterious of all indexes, but is a tremendous resource. The chief benefit of using this index is to be able to sing unfamiliar words with a tune which the congregation knows.

This index is a list of hymn tunes by meter. Meter is determined by counting the syllables of each phrase of hymn poetry. Count the syllables in each phrase. This indicates the numbers (or initials of SM, CM, LM) in the upper righthand corner of the *Book of Hymns*. The period between the numbers indicates the end of sentences, longer phrases, or thought groupings.

There are three major groups of meters, plus those less common. The three major are common meter (CM) which is 86.86; short meter (SM) which is 66.86; and long meter (LM) which is 88.88. One-third of all hymns use one of these three meters.

The initial D after the different meters listed represents *doubled* (the same meter repeated). Some hymns have refrains and alleluias and are listed that way.

The poetic meter is also noted by the word *trochaic,* which means that there is no pick-up note but the hymn begins on an accented beat. Example: "Love Divine, All Loves Excelling," BOH #283.

The poetic meter of *iambic,* on the other hand, means that there is a pick-up beat; that is, the hymn begins with an unaccented syllable. Example: "Come, Ye That Love the Lord," BOH #5.

Thus, by using the index it is possible to exchange any tunes with the same meter. Any tunes with SM or short meter can be exchanged for any other tune. Any tune with CM or common meter can be exchanged.

Examples: Azmon, the tune for "O For a Thousand Tongues to Sing," #1 BOH, can be substituted for the tune Amazing Grace, tune for "Amazing Grace," BOH #92. They both have the same meter, the same poetic syllables.

This index enables familiar tunes to be placed with words appropriate for a specific service or for a special time.

Cautions:

a. Switching tunes can sometimes be frustrating for persons who read music. Sometimes when using a very familiar "other tune," it is well to print the words in the bulletin.

b. Make sure to create a good marriage between tune and text. Make sure that the tune is suitable to the words of the text. You would not want to use a joyful tune for the words of "O Sacred Head Now Wounded," BOH #418, or a somber tune to the words "Joyful, Joyful We Adore Thee," BOH #38.

c. Sometimes tunes are so closely associated with seasons and with certain hymns that it is difficult to use them out of season or with another text.

d. Sometimes challenge the congregation to try a new singable tune rather than always using the tunes they know!

G. PLACING ANTHEMS IN WORSHIP

Leaders of worship together should read carefully the words of the anthem which is to be sung for a particular Sunday. After reading the text, the anthem should be placed where it fits most appropriately and where it helps to move the service. The anthem can be sung in almost any place in the service. It can be an introit anthem, an anthem of praise, an anthem before or after scripture, a prayer anthem, a preparation for the sermon, as a culmination of the sermon, a benediction anthem, or an offering anthem for the Communion service. The possibilities are unlimited.

Proper placement takes planning, however, and a little time and imagination.

Because the congregation is now the principal singing group, it is not imperative that there be an anthem each Sunday. If the choir has not prepared one that is appropriate, let the congregation do all the singing and use the choir next Sunday!

H. SINGING THE PSALMS

The Psalms have been held in captivity for many years. They have been relegated to responsive readings or being read on a Sunday morning. Traditionally, the Book of Psalms was not only a prayerbook of Israel and the church, but a songbook as well. Israel sang these texts in its worship. The Christian community rapidly adopted the Psalms for both its Sunday worship and its daily prayer. Paul wrote to the churches, admonishing them to sing Psalms, hymns, and spiritual songs.

Fortunately, there has been a tremendous renewal of the singing of the Psalms. You are encouraged to introduce your congregation to this vital and biblical sung prayer.

In the Word and Table pattern, the Psalms function as the response of the people to the hearing of the first lesson. With this use in mind, the lectionary Psalm of the day has been selected in relationship to the themes and images of the Old Testament lesson. Such Psalms are not another "lesson" within this renewed pattern of worship; instead they are the congregation's biblical way of responding in song and prayer to the hearing of God's Word.

Psalms may be sung by the people using an antiphon, a hymn setting, or a through-composed choral anthem setting. To use an antiphon, see *Psalms for Singing* or *alive now!* July/August 1981 issue, "Singing Our Prayers." There are many settings of Psalms with the antiphons written for use with a congregation. Almost any musician with a little knowledge of musical writing could write antiphons for the Psalms not used in this particular publication. And there are now Psalm settings published by different denominations for all the Psalms. (See *The Psalmody for the Day,* Series A, B, C, Fortress Press. Permission can be secured for using anything copyrighted by Fortress Press to use in the bulletin. See also *Psalms for Singing* (The Upper Room, 1984).

Many of our hymns are based on Psalms or are paraphrases of Psalms. Look at Index #847, Index of Scripture References of Hymns. By far the largest group of hymns based on scripture is that based on the Psalms. They can well be used as responses and aids to worship. Also see Index to *Celebremos II* for Singing the Psalms.

More and more anthems are being composed based on the Psalms—anthems using plainsong, through-composed, or concertatos (the choir and congregation combining in song). Many publishers have large numbers of anthems using the Psalms.

Use your imagination and look for all the new resources to use the Psalms as a songbook and as aids to worship.

94

I. MUSICAL BIBLIOGRAPHY

The Faith We Sing, Paul Shilling, Westminster Press, 1983
Hymns and Their Uses, James Rawlings Sydnor, Agape Press, 1982
Congregational Singing, William J. Reynolds, Convention Press, 1975
Sing with Understanding, Harry Eskew and Hugh T. McElrath, Broadman Press, 1980
Ministry and Music, Robert H. Mitchell, Westminster Press, 1978
Music in Your Church, William C. Hunter, Judson Press, 1981
Faithsong, Thomas Are, Westminster Press
Companion to the Book of Hymns; Gealy, Lovelace, and Young; Abingdon, 1970
Companion to the Book of Hymns Supplement, Braun, Discipleship Resources, 1983
The Gospel in Hymns, Albert Bailey, Charles Scribner's Sons, 1950
A Joyful Sound Christian Hymnody; Reynolds and Price; Holt Rinehart Winston, 1978
Psalms for Singing, The Upper Room, 1984
The Psalms: A New Translation for Prayer and Worship, The Upper Room, 1984

VIII. CHILDREN IN WORSHIP

The church at worship must recognize each child as a unique individual, help each one belong, and allow each child to participate actively, thereby enabling both children and adults to grow in grace and faith.

The goal of including children in worship is to help them perceive, organize, and interpret the world as Christians by . . .

1. Having the freedom to articulate their own view of the world;

2. Learning how to use concrete religious language in simple, declarative sentences that avoid relational, complex, and metaphorical language;

3. Having opportunities to experience all aspects of worship; and

4. Being able, within their limited experience, to imitate behavior consistent with the Christian faith.

See:

• P. W. McLarty, *The Children, Yes!* (Nashville: Discipleship Resources, 1981)

• W. Willimon, *Keep Them in Their Place* (Worship Alive Series, Discipleship Resources)

• D. Ng and V. Thomas, *Children in the Worshiping Community* (Atlanta: John Knox, 1981)

• V. C. Thomas, *Worship Readiness: Preparing Children for Congregtional Worship* (Worship Alive Series, Discipleship Resources)

These periodicals may aid in the ministry to children:

• *Pockets* (a publication of The Upper Room for children)

• *Brethren House Times* (Church of the Brethren publication for children; 6301 56th Ave., N., St. Petersburg, Florida 33709)

• *Children in the Faith Community Sample Packet* (0212P, Discipleship Resources). A series of ten leaflets suitable as bulletin inserts describing the place of children in the church, with specific suggestions.

GENERAL PRINCIPLES

Encourage families to pray together and prepare for worship together.

Encourage all children, from infants up, to come to worship.

Encourage families to worship together.

Encourage all ages to work together in worship.

Encourage children to participate actively in all worship acts.

In work with pre-schoolers, focus on movement, color, and song.

In work with elementary children—the prime candidates for children's sermons—continue to focus on concrete things and situations.

BEFORE THE SERVICE

Give children a tour of the sanctuary.

Let children help clean and prepare the sanctuary for worship.

Design a bulletin for the children. See V. C. Thomas, *Worship Guides for Children: Adapting the Sunday Bulletin* (Worship Alive Series, Discipleship Resources).

Encourage the children to look up the scripture lessons, prayers, creeds, and hymns.

See the periodical, *Church School Today* (Nashville: United Methodist Publishing House), for lists of children's hymns and anthems that are in the children's literature in Sunday school. These typically correspond to the church year.

A. ENTRANCE AND PRAISE

Encourage children to sing the hymns of praise. Let the children introduce new hymns to the congregation. Help children act out the hymns for the congregation.

Let children process in with banners during the first hymn.

Use banners designed and created by children.

B. PROCLAMATION AND PRAISE

Use children as Bible bearers.

Encourage children to read along with the scripture readings.

Let children read the scripture to the congregation. This requires much practice but is worth the effort.

Have sermons be inclusive of children's needs and experiences at different points throughout.

Children's Sermon or Children's Time

See C. R. Foster, *Proclaiming the Word with Children* (Worship Alive Series, Discipleship Resources).

When used . . .

Sit on the same level with the children.

Talk *with* children, not *at* them.

Not needed on days with Communion or baptism, or in special services where action or drama already provides movement or special involvement.

Be biblical, logical, and clear.

The children's sermon or time should deal with the same text and same central idea as the "other" sermon.

Helpful Ways to Include Children in the Service

1. Storytelling

See E. M. Ward, *Storytelling* (Nashville: Discipleship Resources, 1981); W. R. White, *Speaking in Stories* (Minneapolis: Augsburg, 1982); J. Aurelio, *Story Sunday* (New York: Paulist, 1978).

Storytelling requires much practice with voice, face, gestures, and body.

Three essential steps:

a. Choose a good story: a parable, or other Bible story, a traditional tale, or a personal story. The story should be appealing, enjoyable, suitable, happy, ethical, and appropriate to the scripture and age of the listeners. The story should have a good theme with style, depth of characterization, rhythm, and surprise. Finally, the story should be interesting and within the children's experience.

b. Prepare the story: Know and visualize the story. Read it out loud. Ask its purpose. Outline it. Plan to use props sparingly if at all. Then introduce the story well. Make the plot move. Use direct discourse, with repetition and short sentences. Build to a strong climax.

c. Ending. Do not moralize. The concrete story itself should carry the idea. If you have to explain the story, do not use it!

2. Object Lessons

See E. Weisheit, *To the Kid in the Pew A,B,C* (St. Louis: Concordia, 1975).

If you must explain the object, do not use it. The children simply cannot make such abstract concepts come alive.

Should be based on scripture, not object.

Avoid analogy and metaphors.

Avoid object lesson books that do not list or index the scripture.

3. Experiential Sermon

These sermons live the story. Act out with the children stories such as the lost sheep, leading the blind, and Tower of Babel.

Tour the sanctuary.

Explain the sacraments.

4. Dialogue Sermon

See A. W. Gobbel and R. C. Huber, *Creative Designs with Children and Worship* (Atlanta: John Knox, 1981).

Let the children ask questions, tell stories, and express their own views.

Learn to ask good questions.

5. Children's Time

See J. H. and R. D. Robinson, *How to Involve Children in Worship Services* (St. Louis: Concordia, 1980).

Let the children lead the time by drama, reading, acting, and singing.

6. Story-Hymn

Tell the story of a new or old hymn and sing it with the children.

C. RESPONSES AND OFFERINGS

Have the children usher, receive the offerings, light the candles, carry banners, and lead in prayer.

At the offering, encourage children to place in the collection plate money, a slip of paper pledging a good deed, a slip of paper asking for a special need or expressing a dream or hope. Encourage children also to offer gifts of food or toys for others.

At baptisms, invite the children to come up and see the baptism. Teach the children with *Baptism* multimedia kit. Encourage the baptism of infants of faithful parents.

At Communion, baptized children should come and receive. Use children as servers. Teach the children with *Holy Communion* multimedia kit.

See *Preparing Parents and the Congregation for the Baptism of Infants and Children* (Worship Alive Series, Discipleship Resources).

D. SENDING FORTH

Let the children lead the congregation out.
Let the children greet people as they leave.

IX. MOVEMENT IN WORSHIP

Leaders of worship speak not only through their words but also through their actions. Let each human movement in each service be purposeful, easily seen, unaffected, varied, and appropriate to each aspect of worship.

Use sign language, a beautiful art form, for the deaf and for the whole congregation.

See C. Deitering, *Actions, Gestures, and Bodily Attitudes* (California: Resource Publications, 1980).

A. SUGGESTIONS FOR ALL LEADERS OF WORSHIP

Study R. Hovda's *Strong, Loving, and Wise* (Washington: Liturgical Conference, 1976).

The best way to develop movement and action is to walk nonverbally through each service and learn how to express each part of the service by movement and action.

Congregations become involved in worship primarily when leaders can bodily express their urge to communicate and can physically show their intent.

The Voice

Speak clearly, emphasizing the right words.

Always follow the patterns of the text read and let the text speak through the reader, while also being faithful to oneself and to one's own gifts.

Vary the tone, speed, and cadence of words.

Good sermon presentation demands that each preacher: write out the full sermon; then outline the major points; then practice, practice, and practice, using outline; then speak without the use of the outline; then tape the sermon and listen to the presentation.

The Face

Let your face tell the story.

Look at the people.

Look interested in and look at the other actions of worship. Ministers should not read the bulletin or sermon during the anthem. Ushers should sit still and listen. Choirs should focus on the preacher during the sermon.

Move one's gaze slowly across the sanctuary.

Do not bury your face in the Bible, sermon, or bulletin.

Sing hymns enthusiastically.

The Posture

Be yourself yet invest your body in worship.

Be hospitable.

Be reverent.

Kneel for confessional prayer; stand for prayers of thanksgiving.

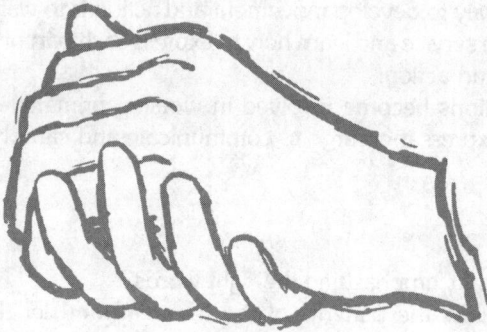

The Actions

Be a representative of the whole congregation, yet do not dominate all actions.

Be visible; do not hide behind the pulpit or lectern.

Use broad movements that are not jerky or sharp.

Keep things moving, but do not be too efficient. Do not walk around or shuffle papers during an end of an anthem, hymn, Gloria Patri, or Doxology.

Keep hands clear; put down hymnals, paper, and bulletin.

Handle the pulpit Bible with care, but do not be sentimental.

Move intentionally during transitions, but do not move too quickly.

In prayer, stand with hands upraised for praise, and kneel for confession.

Be tactile in the sacraments. At a baptism, use a great deal of water and get the candidate wet. Lay hands on the candidate with force. At Communion, visibly break the bread, lift the cup, and touch the people while distributing.

B. SUGGESTIONS FOR OTHER WORSHIP LEADERS

Acolytes: Helpers in Worship

See F. A. Riddle, *Acolyte Training* (Worship Alive Series, Discipleship Resources).

A good use of children in worship.

Be intentional, well paced, and respectful.

Help lead congregational actions.

Assist at baptisms by holding water.

Assist at Communion by distributing elements.

Greeters: Hosts at Worship

Be warm and strong in welcoming members and visitors.

Be alert and intentional to help with special needs.

Ushers: Doorkeepers at Worship

See K. M. Johnson, *Church Ushers* (Pilgrim Press, 1982).

See E. L. Crump, *The Ministry of Ushering* (Worship Alive Series, Discipleship Resources).

Use children, youth, and adults of all ages and sexes.
Help prepare the sanctuary for worship.
Assist the acolytes.
Be personable and warm.
Help lead congregational actions.
Lead the congregation in singing the Doxology.
Distribute the Communion elements to those unable to come and receive.
Bring in the Communion elements with the offering.

Organists and Pianists

Be strong in your leadership of hymns. Do not be timid.
Do not let the congregation lead you in the tempo.
Be interested in the whole service, not only the music.
Take an active part in the responses.
Understand the whole scope of the worship service, not just the music.

Choir Directors

Sing with enthusiasm and a smile.
Be interested in the total worship service.
Do not talk in the choir during the service.
Communicate to the congregation the importance of music.
Understand the whole scope of the worship service, not just the music.

Choir

Sing with enthusiasm when leading the congregation in hymn singing.
Sing from the center aisle, or from among the congregation, or antiphonally from the back or front of the sanctuary.
Do not talk and move around during the service.

C. SUGGESTIONS FOR THE CONGREGATION

Explore various congregational movements as responses to the Word.
Make provision for persons with handicapping conditions and older persons in order not to exclude them from any act of worship.

Make motions reasonable; do not sit or stand too long, or be up and down all service long.

Be sure to give adequate space, time, and opportunity for people to respond.

1. *Entrance and Praise*

Process into the sanctuary on Palm/Passion Sunday and at other times.
Stand for prayers of praise, call to worship, and hymns.

2. *Proclamation and Praise*

Stand for the Gospel reading or for all the readings, or for the primary text of the day.
Use liturgical dance.
Encourage readers' theater on Palm/Passion Sunday.
Practice religious drama. See below for suggestions.

3. *Responses and Offerings*

Ask for physical responses to the Word: raise hand, come forward, use pew for prayer, pass the peace both verbally and nonverbally, use silence, and stand or kneel for prayer.

Receive the Lord's Supper as the best physical response to the Word.

Invite people to come and renew their baptismal vows in *A Service of Baptism, Confirmation, and Renewal* by touching the water or being sprinkled by the water.

Use liturgical dance to tell stories, parables, biblical themes, or themes for the day. Use the action to express thoughts or feelings, as well as stories.

Use follow-the-leader dance and let the children follow and lead dance movements.

See R. B. Branigan's *Forming Dance Choirs, Dance Ministry to Special Persons,* and *Dance in Worship and Ministry*—leaflets in the Worship Alive Series (Discipleship Resources).

See M. G. Taylor, *A Time to Dance* (Austin: Sharing Company, 1981).

4. *Sending Forth*

Sing and process out. Process out especially on the Day of Pentecost.

D. DRAMA AND WORSHIP

Use drama in worship and at youth retreats, choir retreats, church retreats, and at Sunday school.

Present drama as sermon starters, sermons, or as responses to sermons.

Use in the sanctuary, the fellowship hall, or outside.

Use drama in every season of the church year, not just at Christmas or Easter.

Types of drama

Full-length plays, both sacred plays and secular plays, with religious themes.

Short excerpts from full-length plays.

"Stingers"—short, sharp skits (without sets, costumes, or props) that evoke one idea or feeling.

Sounds alone, such as the cry of a baby, a cock crowing, or the sounds of a whip.

Shadow shows.

Musical dramas.

Pantomime.

Role playing.

Monologues.

Clowns and clowning.

Poetic reading.

Plays written by local church members.

Resources

- Contemporary Drama Service
  Box 457-LC
  Downers Grove, Illinois 60515

- C.S.S. Publications
  628 South Main Street
  Lima, Ohio 45804

- Lillenas Musicreations
  Box 527
  Kansas City, MO 64141

X. THE ENVIRONMENT OF WORSHIP

The setting of each service of worship—the church grounds, sanctuary, altar/table settings, lights, and clothing—may enhance worship. Use the environment and do not let it use you. The key to success is to integrate the environment with the scripture lessons and the responses of the people. In general, always keep the worship space uncluttered; use and focus on just a few good things.

See M. K. Nimocks, *Visuals in Worship* (Worship Alive Series, Discipleship Resources).

Secure C. A. Kapikian's *Through the Christian Year: An Illustrated Guide* (Nashville: Abingdon, 1983), a beautiful book of illustrations that may help guide plans for banners.

See Hoyt Hickman's *United Methodist Altars* (Abingdon, 1984) and Diedra Kriewald's *Vesting the House of the Lord* (Worship Alive Series, Discipleship Resources).

A. VARIOUS SUGGESTIONS

Rope off rear seating areas and have everyone sit together to increase intimacy.

Vary the colors of the paraments (cloth hangings), vestments (ministerial clothing), and banners (cloth hangings) according to the scripture lessons and season of the church year.

Keep the baptismal font visible and central at all times.

Keep the Communion table visible and central at all times.

Use special altar/table settings: deserts at Advent, nativity scenes at Christmas, lights at Epiphany, dead flowers at Lent, many flowers and paschal candle at Easter, red flowers at Pentecost, candles at All Saints', and cornucopia at Thanksgiving.

Burn incense, especially frankincense and myrrh on the Day of Epiphany.

Worship outside during spring, summer, and fall.

Use pictures or small statues.

Use a Christ candle at baptisms.

Use slides on the back wall of the sanctuary.

Show movies and filmstrips.

Use indigenous objects: seashells at the beach, rocks in the mountains, or local produce or products.

Explore all the visual arts: drawing, macramé, film, painting, printmaking, weaving, stitchery, jewelry, pottery, sculpture, collage, mixed media, appliqué, needlepoint, batik, photography, calligraphy, and stained glass.

Use the visual arts in the narthex or other popular area. Change the display frequently.

Have contests for the use of the visual arts, choosing one medium at a time. Let everyone be a winner.

Always make sure that the environment of worship is accessible to all persons, regardless of disabilities.

B. BANNERS

These decorative wall hangings may be carried, placed on a stand, or hung next to a wall. They are an excellent way to change the environment and to express the theme of a season, a particular day, a special interest, a creed, a covenant, or a hymn.

Encourage children, youth, and adults of all ages to create the banners.

Focus on color, shape, and texture rather than elaborate and complex symbols.

Avoid the excessive use of words.

Use an opaque projector to transfer patterns to material. Fabric crayons are excellent for outlining patterns.

Avoid spending too much money on a banner unless it will be used often and properly stored. Wool and rip-stop nylon are good materials for permanent banners. Avoid felt and glue for permanent banners. Often the best banners are made with inexpensive material, then used for one service and thrown away.

Hang banners away from walls in order to let them move with air currents.

The best banner book is M. C. Blair and C. Cyan, *Banners and Flags* (New York: Harcourt, Brace, Jovanovich, 1973). Also see:

• B. Wolfe, *The Banner Book* (Wilton: Morehouse-Barlow, 1974)

- L. A. Raynor and C. H. Kerr, *Church Needlepoint* (Wilton: Morehouse-Barlow, 1976)
- E. Lauckner, *Signs of Celebration* (St. Louis: Concordia, 1978)
- J. Marxhausen, *See His Banners Go* (St. Louis: Concordia, 1975)
- D. Kriewald, *Vesting the House of the Lord* (Nashville: Discipleship Resources, 1983)
- M. K. Nimocks, *Visuals in Worship* (Nashville: Discipleship Resources, 1983)

For additional help, write:

- Susan Edenborough
  31 Alvarado Rd.
  Berkeley, CA 94705

- Modern Liturgy
  P.O. Box 444
  Saratoga, CA 95071
  (This organization provides monthly banner suggestions.)

- Designer Banners
  355 Caldwell Circle
  Athens, GA 30605

C. FLOWERS

See O. S. Moffitt, *Arranging Flowers for the Church* (Philadelphia: Fortress, 1977).

Flowers must be subservient to the cross. They should not be higher than the cross, touch the cross, or hide the cross.

Limit the use of flowers.

Eliminate flowers from the Communion table, especially on days of Communion.

Use indigenous flowers rather than elaborate and costly arrangements.

The best shapes of flower arrangements are round, saucer-shaped, bell-shaped, clustered, spiked with flowers, and balls. Establish contrasts between shapes.

The most balanced flower arrangements are triangles, ovals, and vertical.

Be simple rather than elaborate. Let the flowers accent, not dominate, the worship space.

D. VESTMENTS

This clothing worn by ministers and other leaders of worship adds significantly to the environment of worship.

Ministerial Vestments

The use of ministerial clothing varies greatly, according to clerical and congregational preference. Currently, ministerial clothing ranges from informal clothing to robes to cassocks and surplices.

An alb (simple white robe with sleeves) may be the superior ministerial clothing. A chasuble (garment worn over the alb) gives color and added significance on days with the Lord's Supper.

Use stoles (scarves of cloth worn over the shoulders). Emphasize color and texture rather than elaborate symbols.

Choir Vestments

While there are numerous styles, strive for simplicity, uniformity, and neutral colors that may be accented with stoles of colors that correspond to the season of the church year.

Resources on Vestments

- Paraments and Church Furnishings Catalog
  Cokesbury
  P.O. Box 801
  Nashville, Tennessee 37202

- C. M. Almy Catalog (beautiful vestments)
  37 Purchase Street
  Rye, New York 10581

- Doser Designs (needlepoint)
  605 South Poplar Street
  Lincolnton, North Carolina 28092

- *Fabric Appliqué for Worship* by R. Jerdee
  (Minneapolis: Augsburg, 1982). A beautiful and simple technique
  explained and illustrated.

E. RECOMMENDATIONS FOR THE CHURCH ENVIRONMENT

Advent: Christ Is Coming—Sunday on or after November 27 to December 24

Use purple, blue, gray, or dark paraments, stoles, and banners.
Use rough textures.
Avoid flowers.
Use greenery.
Erect Chrismon tree. Save the trunk for a Lenten cross.
Hang an advent wreath.
Altar/table settings: root, plumb line, trumpet, star of David, messianic rose, blooming desert, desert scene, tree of Jesse, star of Jacob, or fleur-de-lis.
Explain to the congregation why symbols are used.

Christmas: Jesus Christ Is Born—December 25 (or Christmas Eve) to January 6 (or first Sunday of the new year)

Use white or gold paraments, stoles, and banners. Use the finest cloth.
Hang a star.
Continue to use Chrismon tree.
Place wreaths on church doors.
Use lots of candles.
Set up a crèche (nativity scene). But do not include magi (wise men) until the Day of Epiphany (January 6 or first Sunday of the new year).
On the Day of Epiphany, use white paraments, stoles, and banners. Light many candles. Present the gifts of the magi. Burn frankincense and myrrh.

Sundays after Epiphany: Christ Is the Light of the World—January 7 (or the first Sunday after Epiphany) to the last Sunday before Lent

Use green paraments, stoles, and banners, except the first and last Sundays when white is appropriate.
Use indigenous flowers.
Light many candles.
Altar/table settings: water jars.

Lent: Jesus Christ Suffers and Dies—Seventh Wednesday before Easter to the Saturday before Easter Day

Use dark, somber colors—violet, red, or black—on rough cloth for parament, stoles, and banners. Use red stitching.
Erect a large, rough, wooden cross (4' x 6') made from the Chrismon tree.
Hang a veil over the cross.
Remove all shiny objects from the sanctuary.
Avoid the use of flowers.
Hang banners showing the stages of Jesus' passion.
Altar/table settings: costly perfume, coins, whip, crown of thorns, torn garment, nails, spear, sponge, and broken reeds.

Palm/Passion Sunday

Begin the service with deep red or purple paraments, stoles, and banners.

Process with palms. Save the palms to be burned and used as ashes on the following Ash Wednesday.

Altar/table settings: Continue the Lenten symbols of the Passion.

Holy Monday, Tuesday, and Wednesday

Use dark and solemn colors, especially black and red. Each day the colors should become darker by use of cloth overlays.

Avoid the use of flowers.

Altar/table settings: Continue the Lenten symbols of the Passion.

Maundy Thursday

Use dark and somber colors for paraments, stoles, and banners. Use rough fabric.

Avoid using flowers.

Set the altar/table with lighted candles for the Tenebrae service.

Strip the sanctuary at the end of the service, except for the large, wooden cross.

Good Friday

Focus on large wooden cross.

Leave sanctuary stripped.

Holy Saturday

Focus on cross.

Sanctuary remains stripped.

Easter Day

Use white or gold colors on the finest fabric for the paraments, stoles, and banners.

Decorate the sanctuary with shiny objects.

Light many candles. Use paschal candles.

Use beautiful flowers, such as Easter lilies or other white flowers.

Easter: Jesus Christ Lives—Fifty days that begin on the Day of Easter

Use white paraments, stoles, and banners.

Light many candles. Continue to burn the paschal candles until Ascension Day.

Use many beautiful flowers.

On the Day of Pentecost, focus on the baptismal font; use red flowers; make banners with doves, flames of fire, or birthday cake; place on the altar/tables signs of the congregation's gifts.

Sundays after Pentecost—the first Sunday after the Day of Pentecost to the last Sunday before Advent

Coordinate the colors and fabrics of the paraments, stoles, and banners of the day. Use the color green except on Trinity Sunday, All Saints', and Christ the King when white is appropriate.

Use indigenous flowers.

Altar/table settings should reflect the scripture and human response of the day.

All Saints' Day

Use the best paraments, stoles, and banners. Light many candles. Display beautiful flowers. Display the names of the saints.

Thanksgiving Day

Use cornucopia.

XI. PREPARATION FOR CHANGE

Changes in worship should involve careful planning, executing, and evaluating. The minister has primary responsibility to initiate, plan, recruit, train, and guide liturgical change. But, if reform and renewal are to occur, the minister must involve every leader of worship—the musicians, choir directors, singers, ushers, readers, acolytes, altar guild members, worship committee members, Communion stewards—as well as the whole congregation. Not all of the suggestions offered in this handbook can or should be used in any one congregation. The worship leaders and the congregation may decide together what changes to make and how to implement them. Then every leader of worship can actively and enthusiastically lead the congregation in liturgical changes. And always, the leaders and congregation need to evaluate and refine the changes.

Finally, do not be frightened of change. If worship leaders are sensitive, prayerful, wise, and reverent, they can lead worship reform and make worship the very center of congregational life.

A. FIVE ESSENTIALS FOR CHANGES IN WORSHIP

1. *Strong Leadership:* Leaders Must Lead.

All leaders of worship—ministers, musicians, choir directors, singers, ushers, readers, acolytes, altar guild members, worship committee members, and Communion stewards—need to know the reasons for and goals of worship. Study together and plan together at a worship retreat for the leaders, and then give guidance to the congregation.

See *Worship: Guidelines for Leadership in the Local Church: 1985-1988* (Nashville: United Methodist Publishing House, 1984).

Order the Worship Alive packets of leaflets for pastors, worship work area, Christian educators, and persons with music responsibility (Discipleship Resources).

Use W. Willimon, *Word, Water, Wine, and Bread* (Valley Forge, PA: Judson, 1980). This is an easy history of worship and liturgical theology that provides excellent resources for worship studies by lay people.

Ministers should study J. White, *Introduction to Christian Worship.*

2. *Good Teaching:* Explain the Function of Worship.

Teach about worship in confirmation classes, Sunday school classes, and special study classes; through sermons; in courses for musicians, choir directors, readers, acolytes, ushers, altar guild members, worship committee members, and Communion stewards; at choir rehearsals; in pre-baptismal and pre-marital counseling sessions; and in funeral preparations.

3. *Extensive Plans:* Plan a Whole Year in Advance.

A full year of services, sermon emphases, new orders of worship, and new worship ideas should be outlined and coordinated in order to offer clarity and consistency.

Use the United Methodist Worship Planning Calendar (Abingdon). This calendar helps in planning all services of the year.

4. *Congregational Support:* Everyone Should Know How Worship Will Change and Why.

Let the whole congregation know the anticipated changes and teach them how to be involved in the changes. Provide special song services to introduce new hymns and music. Provide opportunities for the congregation to learn about the role of worship. Provide ways for each person to be more actively involved in worship.

5. *Intentional Worship Structure:* Make All Church Gatherings a Worship Opportunity.

Look at every gathering of the congregation, whether business or pleasure, and infuse a worship pattern into each gathering. Learn how to make each time of gathering an expression of and formative for congregational worship. The goal is to make the whole life of a congregation an activity of worship.

B. ONE STRATEGY FOR CHANGE

This may well work in any size United Methodist church.

1. Plan changes with the leaders of worship at a worship retreat. For example . . .

a. Talk about the function and goal of worship;
b. Evaluate past worship experiences;
c. Begin focusing on the following:

- The church year. Start by emphasizing Lent/Easter/Pentecost because it is the center of the church year. Then emphasize Advent/ Christmas/Epiphany because it is the second great cycle.
- The Word of God. Begin to plan sermons, hymns, prayers, and anthems for each week around the scripture lessons.
- The hymns of the church. Use a hymn survey.
- The sacraments.
- A new pattern of worship.
- The role of music, children, movement, and environment.

2. Advise the official groups of the church about anticipated changes. The Administrative Council (or the Council on Ministries and Administrative Board) should discuss and adopt the plans.

3. Expose the people to the anticipated changes through preaching, teaching opportunities, and singing events. Before using a new form in worship, distribute copies of the new services one month prior to use.

4. Execute the plans with prayerful and well-rehearsed actions, actively involving all the worship leaders and the whole congregation.

5. Evaluate. Rejoice in successes and amend mistakes.

XII. RESOURCING ORGANIZATIONS

All ministers and musicians in The United Methodist Church may join . . .

The Fellowship of United Methodists
in Worship, Music, and the Other Arts
Jerry W. Henry
P.O. Box 6867
North Augusta, South Carolina 29841

This organization sends monthly newsletters about worship and music and sponsors a biennial convocation for United Methodists interested in worship.

Musicians may join the professional organization for organists and choral directors:

The American Guild of Organists
815 Second Avenue, Suite 318
New York, New York 10017

Ministers and musicians may join . . .

The Hymn Society of America
Wittenberg University
Springfield, Ohio 45501

People working with children's choirs will want to join . . .

Choristers Guild
2834 W. Kingsley Road
Garland, Texas 75041